LIVE
HAPPY

LIVE HAPPY

The Best Ways to Make Your House a Home

Kortney & Dave Wilson

PHOTOGRAPHY BY MICHAEL RILSTONE

Collins

HarperCollins Publishers Ltd
Bay Adelaide Centre, East Tower
22 Adelaide Street West, 41st Floor
Toronto, Ontario, Canada
M5H 4E3

www.harpercollins.ca

All photos are by Michael Rilstone, except those on pages 7, 21, 31, 80–81, 83, 100, 101, 123, 126, 129,
132, 142, 167, 204 (bottom photo), 225, 229, 249, 253, 254, 275, 279, 279, 280–81, and 304, which are by
Showcase Photographers; pages 59, 63, 99, 172, 182, 217, 232, 234, 235, 242, 270, and 303, which are courtesy
of the author; page 188, by Carolyn Snell; page 204 (top), by Jake Eichorn; page 212, by Nora Canfield.

Oliver typewriter artwork by Jenny Henley, on page 73, appears courtesy of the artist. Both the
1967 Scooter Girls artwork, which appears on page 21, at top, and the *Cat Bird Café* artwork on
page 254 are © Anderson Design Group, designed by Joel Anderson, and used
by permission of www.ADGstore.com.

Library and Archives Canada Cataloguing in Publication
information is available upon request.

ISBN 978-1-4434-5559-6

Printed and bound in the United States of America

LSC/C 9 8 7 6 5 4 3 2 1

For Jett, Sully, and Lennox.
The very best way we know to live happy is to live every day with you.

INTRODUCTION

For us, living happy is all about feeling at home. Not just at home in our *house,* but at home in *ourselves*—in our own skin, in our likes and dislikes, and in the choices we've made along the way.

Though Dave and I flip houses, we didn't set out to write a book about house flipping. And we didn't want to focus exclusively on design. After all, we started flipping houses to supplement our income from our music. I grew to love design only over time.

The design-loving part of me feels inseparable from the part of me that loves making music, and being a mother, and spending time with friends—so I wanted this book to include those things as well.

Rest assured we drop plenty of design knowledge into these pages, but none of it is design for design's sake. It is all in the spirit of the bigger picture—living happy and feeling more at home.

Design is not decorative. It's so much bigger—and better—than that. It's about taking a space and transforming it into a reflection of your true self. It's about aligning your surroundings not only with what you do, but with *who you are.*

When I look around our house, it's not perfect, but it is a perfect reflection of our family. There's a corner for Jett's hockey stick, a well-placed dresser to house Sully's gaming console, a craft stand for Lennox, a docking station for easy access to music, fruit bowls to encourage healthy snacking, one piece of art that came from a dumpster, and another we bought at an art show. Our home is a snapshot of exactly who we are right now. And so is this book.

Instead of chapters, we've decided to serve up a series of tips.

DAVE: *Chapter books make Davey sleepy.*

Many of these tips are about designing your home for the way you live. Designing for routines, cultivating quiet, keeping things tidy.

We talk a lot about style and staging and simplifying your space.

DAVE: *We also talk about chickens and elves and Def Leppard and where to hide the transparent tape so the kids can't find it.*

And—surprise, surprise—we talk a lot about color.

DAVE: *Yes, "we" talk a lot about color.*

We also weave in stories about our family and share bits about our past—where we started and how the heck we got from our career in country music to a real estate career in Music City. We talk about adopting our daughter, parenting sons, embracing life's changes, and learning to let things go. Because all of these things together have taught us to live happy and feel at home—wherever life leads us.

There are plenty of design books out there. Some instructional, some inspirational, and some what you might call aspirational . . .

DAVE: *As in "LOOK AT ALL THE BEAUTY YOU WILL PROBABLY NEVER ACHIEVE, SUCKER."*

This is not one of those books.

While I love to drool over immaculate images of what looks like God's own living room styled by archangels, Dave and I wanted to write a book that was more down-to-earth. So this is real-life stuff. Fun pictures and bite-size bits of inspiration, life hacks and laughs, and the occasional kick in the pants. And reflections on how to live well and love well—in big ways and small.

How to Approach This Book

- **Start anywhere.** We don't expect anyone to read this cover to cover. In fact, we encourage you not to. Flip to any page, dive in, and see what speaks to you. You'll see that we encourage you to approach design—and even life—in much the same way. Don't get hung up on "the best place to start" or the "right" place. Just start somewhere.

- **Do it your way.** Our way is not the only way. We're sharing what has worked for us . . . so far. Our lives are ever evolving; acknowledging that and being flexible enough to adapt is essential to the "live happy" mission. What works for present Kortney might not work for future Kortney—and it might not work for you ever. And that's okay. We want you to take what works and leave what doesn't.

DAVE: *Except for the bit about Def Leppard. Everyone really needs to give Def Leppard a chance.*

- **Be sure to have fun!** We want you to laugh. Seriously. Laugh with us, laugh at us. We don't take ourselves too seriously and neither should you. While I stand by my advice, and express a few strong opinions here and there—

DAVE: *And also there. And there. And on pretty much all the pages that I didn't write.*

—we want this book to feel like we're hanging out together. Not in a classroom where the teacher has all the answers, but on a front porch swing (with amazing coordinating throw pillows), just shooting the breeze and making ourselves at home.

Live happy.

Love,
Kortney & Dave

LIVE NEAR THE ICE CREAM STORE

Y ou're probably familiar with the first rule of real estate: location, location, location. Location has a big impact on property values. How are the schools? Are there similar properties nearby? Is the neighborhood well established or in transition? Is the house on a busy corner or in the middle of a quiet side street? Are there train tracks running through the backyard? All are important considerations. But here's something you might not always think about when it comes to a home's location: *Where is it located in relation to the things* YOU *love?* Family traditions should be considered right alongside bedrooms, school districts, man caves, and other amenities. If you go to the grocery store five times a day, don't move to a neighborhood that's five miles away from the nearest grocery store. Trust me, it will annoy you. It seems obvious, but people tend to be less than realistic about the necessities when shopping for a new home—because they don't

consider their own desires *necessary.* I, for example, can't live without an ice cream shop in walking distance. I don't even like ice cream (I know that makes me an oddball), but Dave and the kids do, and for us, frequent trips to the ice cream shop are a cherished family tradition. In the summer months, when we have friends over for dinner, we'll "cheat" and walk to the ice cream shop for dessert (we have two close by to choose from). It might seem silly to some, and that's okay. We value ice cream, so an ice cream shop increases our home value *to us.*

So what's your thing? Do you love to take walks in the woods? Maybe that perfect house in the city isn't so perfect. Do you loathe lugging a lawn mower? Perhaps that three-acre lot with a sloping backyard is more than you want to take on. Be honest with yourself. Honor what matters to you, and choose a home in *that* location.

STAGE IT FOR YOURSELF

When someone asks me to list their house for sale, I first ask them to give me a tour. Inevitably, they walk through, pointing out all of the things they never got around to doing. The art they didn't hang, the duvet cover they never bought, the blinds they didn't replace, the chrome they never polished. They'll say things like "I know this couch is too big for the room, and you have to squeeze to get around it, but we'll buy something different if it will help us sell the house for top dollar." They know as well as I do that staging highlights the house in the best possible way.

So while I appreciate my sellers' commitment, wouldn't it be nice if they'd made these home improvements for themselves and not the future owners, so they might have had time to enjoy them? That's what I mean when I say "stage it for yourself." I'm not talking about living in a museum or making design decisions that don't work "in real life." I'm talking about making the most of what you've got, so you can love it *while you're living in it*.

This book is chock-full of staging-related suggestions, all of which are intended to help you get the most joy from your home. Don't save them for when it's time to sell; instead, treat yourself to the home of your dreams.

PERFORM A $100 MAKEOVER MIRACLE (page 218)
Staging doesn't have to mean "out with the old, in with the new." Sometimes it's just shifting things around and reintroducing decorative elements you might have overlooked.

DECAFFEINATE YOUR COFFEE TABLE (page 36)
Clutter can be a total deal breaker when it comes to selling a home. Take my advice on coffee tables, then drink a bunch of coffee and repeat in every room.

REMEMBER THE RULE OF THREE (page 70)
The number three is design magic. Learn it, love it, live it.

GET REAL JOY FROM FAKE PLANTS (page 141)
If you want top dollar, show some green. Real or fake, you've got to have greenery in the design when staging a home for sale.

FLOAT THE SOFA (page 255)
Everyone wants to know where exactly the couch will go. Let your staging show the way.

YOU CAN NEVER HAVE TOO MANY BLANKETS (page 162)
Purchase a few throw blankets to soften your space and incorporate a pop of color.

. . . OR STAGE IT TO SELL

If you are preparing to sell, staging takes the guesswork out of where things should go. It makes use of seemingly useless spaces. And it rightsizes furniture and accessories to maximize comfort. Staging is not about *tricking* the prospective buyer or covering up what's wrong with a house; it's about showing off what works and painting a picture of what it might feel like to live there. And if it feels right? The house will typically fetch top dollar.

Case in point: I have showed houses where two units are mirror images of each other, one staged, the other not. I always show the un-staged side first. Even if the buyer likes it, they often have questions about how it would feel furnished and where things would go.

When I show the staged side, their eyes light up. They say things like "I love the sofa there!" and "That piece of art over the fireplace is amazing." Or "I never would have thought to put a round table in the dining room, but I love it." Staging fills in where the imagination leaves off—and gives buyers a glimpse into their ideal future.

MAKE YOUR FRONT DOOR A HIGH FIVE

I love colorful homes. In Nashville's historic neighborhoods, I'm always noting the creative color combinations people choose.

DAVE: *Is "noting" the same as "judging"?*

KORTNEY: *No. It's not judging. I'm just making mental notes.*

DAVE: *Do your mental notes have letter grades scribbled at the top in red pen?*

KORTNEY: *Sometimes.*

DAVE: *Then you're judging.*

KORTNEY: *Well, you're judging me for judging. Which is even worse!*

DAVE: *How so?*

KORTNEY: *Because you're doing it OUT LOUD. In a book. And I was doing it privately, on teeny-tiny sticky notes in my mind.*

To be fair, when it comes to color, people are proably going to—no, *will*—judge your choices. We humans are hardwired to have strong opinions about color, which shows you just how powerful and transformational a tool it can be.

While it's impractical to repaint the whole house, freshening up the front door color can have a similarly transformative effect, for a fraction of the cost. That's why I advise clients and friends to change it up from time to time, especially when change is just one quart of paint away. So don't overthink it. If you have a passion for purple, paint the front door purple! The neighbors will get over it. (Or not! Who cares?) It's your front door, and it should be a reflection of *you*.

My Favorite Color Guidelines

Color is great. Color coordination is better.
If your house is a neutral color (gray, black, white, beige, and anything in between), you can paint your front door pretty much any shade under the sun. Just be sure to coordinate the other elements as well. I'm talking porch

pillows, potted plants, and summer blooms, as well as shutters, gutters, and trim. If, on the other hand, your home has a bold facade—like colorful clapboard, siding, or brick—think of the front door as an anchor for all of that color and choose a darker shade of the same—or a neutral, like black or gray.

Don't go too hot or too cold. If you're not a fan of pairing neutrals with bright color accents, keep this tip in mind. Warm tones (reds, yellows, and oranges) should be paired with cool tones (blues, greens, and purples) to balance the exterior palette. For example, as much as I love reds and yellows, I would avoid pairing a red house with a yellow door (or vice versa), whereas a red brick house with a navy blue door is right up my alley.

Remember the roof. A roof is a roof is a roof, right? Wrong. People often forget that roof shingles come in a variety of shades. If your shingles have a greenish tinge, that cherry-red door could make your house look like an offshoot of Santa's workshop all year long. So don't forget to take in the *whole* picture. Step back and see your house from the curb, then make a mental note of all of the colors coming into play.

Some Color Pairings I Love

FOR THE WHIMSICAL SPIRIT
- Light pink body. Emerald green door. Creamy gray or ivory trim.

- Chartreuse body. Coral door. Bright white trim.
- Mint green body. Electric blue door. White trim.

COLORLESS, CLASSIC, AND PROUD
- Creamy white body. Light taupe door. Dark taupe or black trim.
- Black body. Stained wood door. White trim.
- White body. White door. White trim. (Choose all different finishes and sheens and this will work until the end of time.)

BOLD BUT NOT RISKY
- White body. Sun yellow door. Light blue porch ceiling. White trim.
- Light gray body. Purple door (any shade). Off-white trim.
- Black body. Black trim. Black door (with full glass). (Dark? Yes. But in the moodiest modern way. I love this look, which works best when the landscape is lush and green.)

LOVERS OF WHITE SPACE
- White body. Bright yellow door. Black trim and gutters.
- White body. Cobalt blue door. White trim and white accents. (Let the door do the talking.)
- White body. Fuchsia door. Black accents.
- White body. Fire-truck red door.
- Creamy off-white body. Robin's-egg blue door. Bright white trim. Black and white accents.

ONE-UP THE WELCOME MAT

I am a total sucker for a charming welcome mat. Yes, they are a bit pricier than their practical grass-mat cousins, but if they make me chuckle every time I enter the house, I consider it a solid return on investment.

DAVE: *Do you remember that welcome mat you bought that said, "Hey, I'm Mat!"*

KORTNEY: *Yes! That's what got me hooked. You didn't think that was funny?*

DAVE: *It was, like, one-"ha" funny. But you would giggle like a litter of baby clowns every time we walked up to the house.*

KORTNEY: *Like a litter of baby clowns? You're exaggerating.*

DAVE: *I wish I was.*

Seriously, though. Our home is the hub for the neighborhood kids. Several of them have their own codes to our house, so I depend on that *hilarious* $30 welcome mat to dish out the laughs *and* keep out the dirt.

Considerations for Picking the Perfect Welcome Mat

- **Pretty or functional?** Why not both? If you have a covered porch, a machine-washable cotton mat is a great option. Choose a color that complements your door, or, better yet, a pattern, which will hide dirt better than a solid color. If not, stick with weatherproof grass, sisal, or even rubber mats (although I'm personally not a fan of the latter, because they feel like they belong on a car floor, not a porch).

Don't go too small. The length of the mat should be as close as possible to the width of the door opening so that it *matches* the entrance (no less than 90 percent of the width). And if you have a sidelight or two (those pretty windows that frame the sides of the door), you'll want to include those in the door-width measurement. If the mat is too small, it will be dwarfed by the door and diminish the look of your entrance.

Make it your own. Think of a word or phrase that will make you or your family smile (or, better yet, giggle like a litter of baby clowns) and create your own mat. Maybe you have a family motto or silly way of saying hello. You might also consider something sweet and sentimental, like tracings of the kids' hands or feet.

DIY WELCOME MAT

Materials You'll Need
Stencil(s)
Blank coir doormat
Sewing pins
Stencil paintbrush (with tough bristles)
Outdoor acrylic paint

1. Gather your materials.

2. Prepare your stencil. It can be homemade or store-bought, but it needs to be sturdy. As long as it's on card stock or vinyl contact paper, it should work just fine.

3. Place the doormat on a flat surface, in an area where you can work and let it dry.

4. Place your stencil on the mat and secure it with pins. (*Not NAILS, Dave.*) Even if you use sticky vinyl, it likely won't stick that well to the mat, so pins are key.

5. Start painting. Don't skimp. Load up your brush with enough paint that it makes a solid mark without having to rub it in. Imagine that your brush is a stamp, and dab on the paint, pushing it into the fibers, rather than moving the brush back and forth. This will prevent the paint from bleeding underneath the stencil and make for much crisper lines. (Although I've seen this done with sponges, it worked much better for me when I used a stencil brush.) Apply the paint over the entire open area of your stencil, overlapping the edges so you get a sharp line.

6. Resist the urge to peek! You must let the paint dry completely before you remove the stencil. Walk away for a few hours so you don't get tempted.

7. Remove the stencil and welcome your new welcome mat!

LIVE YOUR BEST (FRONT PORCH) LIFE

————

Growing up in Canada, we used our backyards much more than our front porches. Having lived in the South for 20 years, I've grown accustomed to front porch living, and I love it so much I encourage everyone to use their front porches—regardless of climate. It's like having an extra room, even if you have to dress warmly to enjoy it. And it's a great way to be social. If I sit down for more than five minutes, one of my friends will stop by with a latte or a glass of wine and stay for a chat. It's like magic.

> **DAVE:** *You're like the Pied Piper of porches. They flock to you like rats.*

> **KORTNEY:** *Not like rats, Dave.*

> **DAVE:** *Are you kidding? Amanda, with the cheese plates?*

> **KORTNEY:** *Does she know you call her "Amanda with the Cheese Plates?"*

> **DAVE:** *She does now. In fact, here she comes now with a nice spread of Gouda…*

The point is, if I didn't have a place to sit or set down my mug (or Amanda's awesome cheese plates), I would never use the porch.

My Front Porch Guidelines

Treat the outdoors as you would the indoors. With intent. Put things on the porch that you will use and enjoy. Do you like candles or incense? Great. Place some in a holder on a side table, with a stack of your favorite magazines at the foot of the chair. This will encourage you to take a few minutes every once in a while to take a breath and enjoy some fresh air.

Choose furniture that's pretty and practical. I'm not a fan of plastic porch chairs, if for no other reason than that they blow all over the place when the wind kicks up. When I furnish a room—which I consider the front porch to be—I like the furniture to stay put. Heavy pieces made of natural materials tend to stand the test of time, so you won't have to replace them every season. We found a pair of white Adirondack chairs with matching ottomans that are so cute

and comfortable, it's hard to resist a quick sit. Be sure to have *something* to set a drink down on as well. It doesn't have to be fancy. Just a nice flat surface, so you never turn down an opportunity to take your tea or coffee outside. A tiny painted stool or plant stand will do the trick. Dave and I love to entertain, so we have a couple of larger outdoor tables on our porch as well. That way we can just add snacks, a record player or portable speaker, and a pitcher of lemonade, and we have ourselves a party.

Soften the space with an outdoor rug. Acrylic rugs made for the outdoors will bring a nice pop of color—and a homey feel—to the front porch. And while they won't last forever, they're affordable enough that it doesn't break my heart when they do wear out.

Add accent pillows. Playing off one of the colors in the rug, add some accent pillows to your outdoor living room. Outdoor fabrics will last longer and resist mold and mildew. All-purpose fabrics will work great as long as they're washable. If you've opted out on the rug, have fun with patterns and colors that complement the exterior of your home.

Paint the ceiling. Outsiders might not notice, but I assure you, this tiny touch of color makes a big impact on your front porch vibe. It's an old Southern tradition to paint porch ceilings a color called haint blue. This sea-inspired color is said to ward off evil spirits called haints. But whether or not you believe in such things, a blue ceiling makes a lovely extension of the sky and can reflect the light of day a little bit longer into the evening.

Chalk it up. I tried having a chalkboard wall indoors when it was all the rage, but it wasn't a good match for my obsession with keeping things tidy. So I moved it outdoors, where I can love it and leave it (and hose it down when it gets out of hand). This is a great little DIY as well. Consider painting a piece of smooth particleboard or weather-treated HardieBacker cement board and hanging it by the front door. Add some antique doorknobs or hooks on either end to hold pails of chalk, and let your family and friends have at it.

If you can, swing it. If your porch can accommodate a swing, I highly recommend it. Not only is it nostalgic and lovely to look at, but there's just something about sitting on a porch swing that invites intimacy. Maybe it's sitting side by side and rocking in that gentle rhythm that inspires the kind of heart-to-heart chats that make great memories.

DAVE: *Like when we first brought Lennox home.*

KORTNEY: *That's exactly what I was thinking.*

DAVE: *The boys were so little.*

KORTNEY: *And we were all sitting in the swing, rocking her to sleep. And the boys were trying to be so quiet.*

DAVE: *But actually scream-whispering, "WE LOVE YOU, BABY LENNOX."*

KORTNEY: *You'll never forget it, right?*

DAVE: *Nope, never. Porch swings for the win.*

GIVE YOUR HOUSE A NAME

Every time Dave and I flip a house, we give it a name that captures the spirit of the project and helps drive design decisions along the way. Now, when I tell you to give your house a name, I'm not talking about a first name (though I won't stop you from doing that as well); I'm talking about a *descriptive* name, like the Jewel-Tone Gypsy or the Beachcomber's Bungalow.

DAVE: *Or the Whiskey-Addled Hobo.*

KORTNEY: *Or not that.*

DAVE: *I don't know, I kind of like it.*

KORTNEY: *Well, it's definitely more descriptive than the name you picked for that craftsman bungalow.*

DAVE: *You asked what I would name the house, and I named her Pam. It's a good, solid name. But, yes, I understand now that it wasn't what you were looking for.*

We once took on an old Victorian that was different from any project we'd done in the past. I knew almost immediately that I wanted to take it in a bohemian direction, so I named her Vic, the Boho Victorian. It wasn't the most creative name, but I knew exactly what it meant. Spirited colors. Textured fabrics. Mismatched patterns. All with the eclectic blend of historical styles that the Victorian era is known for. Naming a house this way helps you get to know it better. And every decision I made for that design checked back to the name.

The same was true when we took on the Moody Craftsman—a craftsman-style home that was a complete train wreck. Rather than fight its quirky nature, we decided to work with it, and so we named the house accordingly. It was an opportunity to get away from white on white, and really think creatively. We incorporated crafty upcycled projects into the final staging and kept "moody" in mind when selecting rustic wood accents, dark finishes, two-tone trim and walls, and painted ceilings.

DAVE: *I had my doubts about that one. I was afraid it was too brooding and masculine.*

KORTNEY: *I just had a feeling about it. And my instincts did not betray me.*

The end result was *definitely* moody, but potential buyers loved it. In fact, the women liked it even more than the men. We wound up with a full-priced offer and a backup, so whether or not it was everyone's cup of tea, it lived up to its name and made people feel something.

It's also a lot of fun to brainstorm names. At least, I think it is. It's like creating a mood board with your mind. Think of the words and feelings you want your house to evoke, and let your imagination work its magic.

SEE IT BEFORE
YOU START IT

———

Most of us wouldn't set off on a road trip without a GPS or a map, but you'd be surprised how many people embark on a major renovation without giving a thought to interior design. They'll draw up the plans, build out the space, and only then start thinking about decor.

To this day, before I start any renovation project—or even updates in my own home—I put together a vision board, assembling photos and fabric swatches and paint colors until I zero in on a vision or direction for the project. These aren't necessarily the exact elements I'll use, but they're there to inspire my choices and keep me from veering off course.

Sometimes I'll assemble the images online —or on my phone. Other times I'll make my vision board the old-fashioned way, cutting and pasting the inspiration images to a large poster board. Whatever works for you is fine

as long as the images are all in one place and easily accessible. And the pictures can come from anywhere—Pinterest, Google, design magazines, Instagram, whatever you enjoy perusing—there's a ton of inspiration out there to pull from. Your source material doesn't have to be design specific either. I once took a snapshot of a gorgeous bouquet of flowers and it became the basis for an entire living room design. I put that photo in the center of my vision board and built out the colors and textures and shapes around it.

Let's say you're starting a kitchen renovation. Search the Internet for kitchens you like and don't edit yourself just yet. Simply gather all of the images that speak to you and then step back and start asking yourself some questions. What is the common denominator in all of these pictures? An open concept? A particular color? Glass cabinetry? White countertops? Look for those commonalities. They might surprise you. A friend of mine thought she was setting out to design a pristine white kitchen, but when she created her vision board, it was filled with bold-hued cabinets, revealing her hidden desire for a more colorful kitchen. Your results might be a little less dramatic, but still revealing; for example, you might find yourself drawn to all-white kitchens *and one red one*. If you can't shake that image, maybe an all-white kitchen with a bold red accent wall will make you happiest. Next, google "red accent walls" and you might find a fantastic living room design with just the right red to add to your board for further inspiration.

The idea is to collect images without inhibition until you see a pattern emerge. The pattern will reveal your preferences and guide your vision.

I used this process to create a vision board for our backyard makeover and surprised even myself (which is no easy feat these days). Going into the project, I had no intention of building a firepit. There were too many other "must-have" elements that were higher priority. But as I started to gather my inspiration photos, I realized that nearly every one of them had a firepit featured front and center. I tried to cover up the firepit and see if I liked the photo as much without it, but no dice. It turned out the firepit was the focal point I needed to anchor the outdoor design. So, the firepit became the center of my vision board—and I was able to design my perfect backyard around it.

I encourage you to go into the visioning process with an open mind. While you're gathering images, let your eyes and heart love what they love. Pin and paste your pictures with wild abandon and disregard that rational inner voice that doesn't think white cabinets and kids can coexist in the same house. Maybe they can't, but maybe they can. If you censor yourself too soon, you'll never know.

GET ROMANTIC ABOUT YOUR REAL ESTATE AGENT

Whether you're buying or selling your home, I can't emphasize enough how important it is to find the right agent. So many variables go into pricing, marketing, and selling a house, you want to make sure you're hiring a pro, someone you'll be comfortable working with for the long haul. Tempting as it may be to save a few thousand dollars with a private sale, that can wind up being a costly mistake. Say, for example, you find your dream house, with a big backyard that's just perfect for building a pool. You move forward with a private sale, save yourself the agent's commission, and find out—only after the sale has closed—that there's a utility easement straight through the middle of the yard, the only place where that dream pool could conceivably go. A good Realtor would have suggested adding a contingency in the contract to allow you a period of due diligence to make sure the pool was a go. But because you decided to go it alone, you're stuck.

Even when the process moves quickly and everything goes off without a hitch, you'll be spending a lot of time together. I tell friends to think of it as a short marriage (I'm a romantic, what can I say?)—so *choose wisely*. It's great to ask friends for referrals, but don't stop there. Interview a minimum of three agents before you make a decision. (A quick note: While many people use the terms "real estate agent" and "Realtor" interchangeably, they're not the same thing. A Realtor is a member of the Canadian Real Estate Association or the National Association of Realtors in the United States. That means a Realtor is bound by a strict code of ethics and undergoes ongoing training. Long story short: The Realtors I know work their tails off on behalf of their clients. And they know their stuff. Okay, commercial over. Let's find your perfect match.)

Here are the questions to ask during the "speed-dating" round. And if the agent seems flustered by a few rapid-fire questions, you can end the interview right there. Any agent worth her salt is expecting a friendly interrogation. So let's begin.

Questions to Ask Potential Real Estate Agents

Do you sell real estate full-time? Lord knows I love a multitasker, but if your agent is working a desk job (and that desk is not located smackdab in the middle of a real estate office), they *might not* have their finger on the pulse of the market. There are exceptions to this rule, of course. Like, say, the TV host who is also a real estate agent. But keep in mind, I have— I mean *she* has—a team of highly qualified and experienced agents that work for her full-time, because that's what her clients (rightly) demand.

How many sales have you handled in my area in the last 12 months? If the answer is "none in your area, but . . . ," then they might not be a good fit. I've lost listings for this very reason. It stings, because I know that I can get the job done, but I also respect the fact that an agent who works predominantly in that area will have more connections to get the job done right. As for years of experience, I'm less of a stickler. All of us were newbies at one time, and I love an agent who's willing to fake it till they make it. But they still have to know the market inside and out. If you're the seller, they have to understand what local buyers are looking for and price your house appropriately. If you're the buyer, the agent should have an ear to the ground so they know what's coming up. We call these houses pocket listings. They haven't yet hit the market, but they

will soon. Buyers, especially in hot areas, need an agent who is in the know.

How do you like to communicate with your clients? The correct answer is "How would *you* like me to communicate?" Remember what I said about this being a marriage. Poor communication is a relationship killer. And everyone defines poor communication differently. So be honest with your agent and yourself about what good communication looks like. I've had clients who like daily updates and others who would rather not hear from me until there's an offer on the table—even if the house is months on the market. A good agent will accommodate your preferred style of communication, not the other way around.

How will you market my home? Please be specific. Your agent should be well versed in all of the marketing channels available, and that includes social media. They should have a good website. An e-newsletter. And, for the love of Pete, they must take good photos—or hire someone who will. Bad photography is a total turnoff to home buyers. Not only does it fail to showcase your home in the best light, it makes it look like you're out of touch and perhaps unmotivated to sell. So make sure your *agent* is ready for your home's close-up. Ask to see the marketing materials from their last five listings. This will give you a good feel for how they work, *and* it will also ensure that they've *had* five recent listings.

What things can I do to my home right now in order to sell quickly and maximize my profit? Oftentimes sellers are so close to their homes they can't see the tiny flaws or imperfections that buyers will zero in on immediately. A good agent can size up your home, make smart suggestions, and tell you where to focus your energy (and your investment) to maximize returns. A good agent will also ask you to share any hidden value that buyers can't readily see. Maybe you put in fancy insulation (as fancy as insulation can be). Or you just repainted the bedrooms or installed a new faucet in the kitchen. A good agent will ask you to share those upgrades, so she can market them. She might also advise you to write a letter to potential buyers, explaining why you love your house and listing any interesting details or history that might not be obvious to the naked eye.

What things can I do to make my offer sweeter to potential sellers? I always advise my clients to get preapproved for a mortgage and to write a letter about themselves to include in future offers. It's a personal touch that helps the seller envision their home in good hands.

KNOW YOUR PAINT COLOR PERSONALITY

We all have different thoughts and feelings and ideas about color, but when it comes to *painting* with color, I find that people generally tend to fall into one of two categories: "petrified of paint colors" or "can't get enough color."

Petrified of Paint Colors?

If you fall into this category, here's my advice: paint the majority of your interior one neutral color. That's right! Just one. It can be a gray, an ivory, a white, a taupe, or a beige. Yes, there is an overwhelming number of neutrals to choose from. No, you don't have to let that paralyze you. Decide whether you prefer cool tones or warm tones and then . . . *just pick one.* Seriously. As far as I'm aware, no one has ever died of *ecru*, so just dive right in and pick something that appeals to you. Or, if you're so petrified your brain is frozen and you don't know what appeals to you, ask a friend you trust what appeals to them and do whatever they say. Do not overthink it.

And now you're thinking, *But neutrals are so boring. I don't want to be boring!*

You are not boring.
You are fascinating.

DAVE: *You are. Everyone says so.*

So what's a color you love? Red? Orange? Navy? Yellow? Pink? What speaks to your secret heart of hearts? What's the color you'd love to wear *if only you could pull it off*? Pick that color, and find a shade of it that coordinates with your neutral. If you're thinking, *Easy for you to say, Kortney, you're not the one who's petrified of color!*—I've got your back. Take a deep breath and agree to let yourself play a little bit, okay? Instead of taping 10 million paint swatches all over the wall and praying to the color gods to take pity on you, try this instead: go on a treasure hunt. Find some accent pillows or pieces of fabric (or blankets) in *various shades of that awesome color* and just live with them in your space. One of them is going to feel fabulous (maybe all of them will—in which case, you can't go wrong). When you identify a shade you love, take that pillow (or fabric swatch or whatever it is) straight down to the paint store and ask them to match it.

DAVE: *Also? Breathe.*

Now you're going to take that color and paint a small area—like an accent wall, or a door, or the wall of your built-in shelves—in that color.

DAVE: *And breathe again.*

Now put the paint away and repeat that color in little ways throughout other areas of your home. Repeat it with furniture or artwork, hardware or accessories. Repeat it with a throw rug and two matching tea towels. No need to go overboard; just sprinkle that color around and see how the space is transformed.

On previous seasons of our show, we used this very technique, painting all of the walls white except for one small cubby in the kitchen, which we gave a soft petal pink accent. Everyone who came to tour it referred back to it as the "pink house," though the vast majority of the design was neutral. Repetition of one single color, even in small ways, will make a big impression—and make you look color-confident, even when you're petrified of paint.

Can't Get Enough Color?

I feel you, color lovers. I really do. So you may not like what I'm about to tell you.

DAVE: *Do you want me to tell them?*

KORTNEY: *Yes. I'll hide over here.*

DAVE: *RESIST THE RAINBOW, or keep your paws off the paint!*

I know it hurts, but Dave's right. If a variety of colors is what you crave, the paint store is no place for you. Trust me. I have tasted the rainbow. Color lovers are *so* much better off painting the entire house a neutral color and using interchangeable accents to bring color to the fore. Because here's what happens to us color lovers: we get bored easily. And when we try to paint our way out of boredom, our homes can quickly become less Picasso and more Pee-Wee's Playhouse. I tried to sell a house a few years ago in which color had gotten the best of the homeowner. Walking from a purple room, to a blue room, to a green room, to another purple room, the buyers were scared off. Most people just can't see past all that color. When I had the homeowner paint the interior a neutral gray, an offer promptly followed.

Even if you *never* intend to sell your house, you will definitely want to change up the colors—probably more frequently than most. So give yourself the gift of neutral walls and let the rainbow reign through accents and art.

MIX, DON'T MATCH

———

I've never been a fan of "themed" decor. As far as I'm concerned, themes are great for parties and proms, but they tend to be too narrow—and therefore limiting—for interior design. When I'm designing a room from the ground up (or the ceiling down, as the case may be), I like to think in terms of an overarching concept rather than a theme. "Laid-back lake house" is what I consider a concept, whereas "ducks" would be more of a theme. If ducks are your jam, there's certainly room for one or two in a laid-back lake house. For example, a photograph of a duck on a lake could be lovely. But festooning a room with matching duck napkins, duck curtains, and duck pillows . . .

DAVE: . . . *will make you look like a quack.*

I don't mean to disparage duck lovers or minimize anyone's passion for, say, polka dots, but when it comes to cohesive design, more mixing and less matching is key.

If you're that person who's passionate about polka dots, feature them prominently. Find a fabulous polka-dot paper and put it on an accent wall. Or paint the walls white and have a fabulous polka-dot print on the curtains. Whether it's a wall, or curtains, or a piece of furniture with polka-dotted upholstery, I want you to pick one—and only one. Then stop matching and start mixing. If you decided on polka-dot curtains, a throw pillow with a single polka dot would be a nice touch. Perhaps you hang a minimalist watercolor with a circle motif on the wall as well, and choose a round coffee table, instead of a square one. By mixing in these complementary (but not matching) elements, you reinforce your focal point rather than compete with it.

CULTIVATE QUIET

I've created a cozy spot in our home where all three of our children feel so relaxed and content they retreat into happy silence to daydream, read books, or just think deeply about their life's purpose for hours on end. I love this spot. It's one of my greatest masterpieces. I call it *my imagination*. It's like Pinterest, without all the fails. In real Wilson life, however, quiet spaces (at least the ones with kids in them) are few and far between. And for the most part, we like it that way. But! We have found a few clever ways to cultivate calm and quiet in our home, and design (surprise, surprise) can play a big part.

Ironically, our family's chosen quiet spot happens to be our music room, which replaced our formal living room from day one. Dave and I are far more likely to be found playing music than we are to be playing "fancy grown-ups in our fancy living room," so this switch suits us perfectly.

DAVE: *I am actually very fancy. The music room was Kortney's idea.*

KORTNEY: *That's true. Our friends actually refer to him as Fancy Dave.*

While you might not think a room filled with musical instruments (and little hands playing them) could become a quiet oasis, it can—*if* you design it with that in mind.

One way to create a sense of calm is to narrow a room's focus. From the guitars and ukes we have hanging on the wall (all of which are functional, and we invite individuals of all skill levels to play them), to the piano that is the room's centerpiece, it is clear that this space is all about music. Whether you're playing, singing, writing, or listening, having that singular focus, and a room that fosters it, has an instant calming effect.

The view also helps. Instead of a sofa set and a coffee table, the piano is the room's focal point, and it faces a large window with a great view of our street. So even as you're turning inward emotionally, the way music makes you do, you have this visual escape that lets you unplug from the hustle of the house behind you.

DAVE: *Visual escape . . . turning inward emotionally? Look who's fancy now, wife of Fancy Dave. I thought we pointed the piano at the window so we could turn our backs on the kids without being called out for neglect.*

KORTNEY: *No, that's not why.*

DAVE: *So then tell us about the books you have stacked up on the ottoman. Do those also support your emotional journey to inner calm? I just assumed they were there to keep the kids from loitering.*

KORTNEY: *They're totally there to keep the kids from loitering.*

DAVE: *YES. I got one right.*

Now, if anyone wants to recline and revel in the music, we do have two really cool chairs for that. But they're a sidebar to the room, not the main idea. The goal, if you're cultivating quiet and calm, is to allow your space to serve a single purpose—in this case, it's making music. So even though there is sound in the room (which any parent will tell you is *very* different from noise), you can still experience that sought-after peace and quiet.

Your quiet place doesn't have to be a whole room. It could be a prayer closet or a gift-wrapping station or a desk at the top of the stairs. The point is that this is a dedicated space in your home that calls you to stop and enjoy a peaceful moment or two.

HAVE A PLACE TO HIDE

This is the nook at the top of the stairs. Dave wanted to put an accent table there, but at the last minute, I nixed it in favor of something more functional. And lo and behold . . .

DAVE: *Lo and behold . . .*

KORTNEY: *Do you want to say it, or should I?*

DAVE: *I think it goes without saying.*

KORTNEY: *Let's say it together anyway, shall we? I WAS RIGHT.*

Small spaces are another natural way to cultivate quiet in the home, for the obvious reason that only one kid can fit in there at a time. (Of course, when you're calculating your "quiet" return on investment, you can't count the noisy arguing over who's hogging the space.)

Not only do the kids cozy up in here to read (or play video games, let's be real), it's become a secondary sleep spot. Why sleep in your own comfy bed when you can sleep in the hallway, right?

DAVE: *That's one of my mottos.*

Jett's mostly outgrown it, but Sully and Lennox still fight over whose night it is in the nook. And when any one of the kids is sick, they head straight to this little incubator at the top of the stairs until their healthier self is ready to hatch.

DAVE: *Nice chicken metaphor.*

KORTNEY: *Thank you.*

DAVE: *That was clucking amazing.*

KORTNEY: *Oh my god, stop.*

A nook doesn't have to be fancy. A couple of beanbag chairs in a corner of the living room—or a bench beneath the bay window in your kitchen. It could be an oversize chair with plenty of pillows. As long as it's cozy and comfortable, it counts.

DECAFFEINATE YOUR COFFEE TABLE

———

Clutter makes me crazy. This is especially true when it comes to coffee tables, which, even when they're not the focal point of a room, are guaranteed to get a lot of attention. After all, a coffee table (or a cocktail table, as we call it, depending on the time of day) is meant to be practical and functional. But just because something has a few cocktails on it doesn't mean it has to look like a disheveled drunk about to pass out in the middle of your living room. I swear to you, I can hear coffee tables weep beneath the weight of outdated *People* magazines and mismatched novelty coasters.

A coffee table should be an oasis of calm.

DAVE: *Is there any place in the house that shouldn't be an oasis of calm?*

KORTNEY. *No.*

DAVE: *If the whole house is an oasis, then technically . . .*

KORTNEY: *I love you. Be quiet with your pretty lips.*

DAVE: *Got it. Consider me an oasis of calm.*

As I was saying. Stop torturing your coffee tables with all of that clutter! They don't need the stress. And neither do you. (And neither do *I*.) That's why God made trays.

If your coffee table is round, get yourself a square tray. If your coffee table is square, get a round tray. If your coffee table is so covered in cocktail napkins and remote controls that you don't even know what shape it is, get yourself a big old trash bag and just start over. I'll wait.

Alright. Now that you have your tray and the surface of your table is free of debris, you're going to invoke the rule of threes (discussed in a later chapter). Perhaps you have a tidy stack of art books. (Not a tower, a stack.) And a pretty scented candle. And a ceramic pug wearing a ceramic sweater! Can you see it in your mind's eye? It's a work of art unto itself, and life is worth living again.

DAVE: *Are you okay?*

KORTNEY: *I am now.*

FILL THE BUCKET TO KEEP CLUTTER AT BAY

Have I mentioned that clutter makes me crazy? Not miffed. Not annoyed. Not irritable. But CRAZY.

DAVE: *She's understating it.*

When I walk past a room and see an unmade bed, or clothes piled on the floor, or toys tossed haphazardly to the four corners, I have to stop whatever I'm doing and clean it up. This is not the right thing to do, of course. The kids should clean up their own messes. And they *would*, if I could wait, which I can't, because . . . Ding! Ding! Ding! *CRAZY.*

I know I'm not the only one who experiences anxiety over clutter. But I'm definitely the only one in our family, which is tough on all of us. It's not easy for them to live with a neat freak. And it's not easy for me to live with raisins and granola bar wrappers jammed under the couch cushions.

DAVE: *And by "not easy for me," she means "I'm going to kill you all with this vacuum cleaner attachment."*

KORTNEY: *"Kill" is a strong word.*

DAVE: *And yet somehow, when you're wielding that vacuum hose, it feels like the right word.*

KORTNEY: *I can't help myself.*

To ease everyone's suffering, we've come up with many of the life hacks in this book—from storing things in plain sight to identifying a drop spot. We also have an expression in our family that helps remind the kids that keeping the house clutter-free is a team effort.

DAVE: *"When you cry, we try?"*

KORTNEY: *[silence]*

DAVE: *Did I say that out loud?*

KORTNEY: *That may be your expression, but I was referring to "fill the bucket."*

For the kids, filling the bucket means making

your bed every morning and doing your own laundry. It means taking your turn clearing the table and putting the dishes in the dishwasher. It means keeping your room neat and your stuff put away. Want a ride to the movies Saturday night? No problem. I'll even pay for your ticket and popcorn. But first, do your part to contribute to the family and our household in a meaningful way.

DAVE: *And by "meaningful way," she means "pretend you work for Merry Maids."*

It's not magic by any means, but setting clear expectations and having natural consequences when they're not met definitely helps maintain a sane environment most of the time.

Of course, decluttering is a journey—not a destination. And sometimes "filling the bucket"

means literally *filling a bucket* with all of the stuff you just don't need anymore. No matter how strict I am about what comes through the door, stuff still has a way of piling up like a season of *Unsolved Mysteries*. Even socks without mates are perfectly capable of reproduction. They're like amoebas. Clothes you did not purchase for your children *will* appear on their backs, and in their backpacks, and in backpacks that are not even their backpacks but are nevertheless slung over your entranceway banister like a couple of three-toed sloths.

And now I'm hyperventilating.

DAVE: *I'll get you a paper bag to breathe into.*

KORTNEY: *I think I'm going to need something bigger. Like a bucket.*

HONOR THE HEIRLOOMS

—

Family heirlooms can pose a special challenge for us clutter busters. A home has only so many square feet, and if it's all the same to Dave's late great-granny, I'd rather not dedicate any of them to her collection of bronzed baby shoes. However. There are times, believe it or not, when I'm willing to bend the aesthetic rules for the love of family.

DAVE: *There are?*

KORTNEY: *Are you kidding?*

DAVE: *Almost all the time. But not now. Tell me about these rules you're willing to bend. I'm going to take notes.*

Years ago, when Jett and Sully were babies, Dave's mother came to visit and brought a box of . . . *valuables* . . . to pass down to us.

DAVE: *My Most Improved Player hockey trophy?*

KORTNEY: *That was one of the items, yes.*

One of the other items was an antique washbasin and porcelain bathing pitcher, which was clearly of significant value to Dave's mom.

DAVE: *Let me guess. Not your style?*

KORTNEY: *Not at all.*

But I knew these items were in our lives to stay.

DAVE: *And by "in our lives," you mean "in the basement."*

KORTNEY: *Exactly. Except when your mother would come to visit.*

Over the years, it became a family ritual. When Dave's mom was coming to town, up came the heirlooms and hockey trophies, which we'd prominently display. And it made her so happy to see these things, and see that we

appreciated them, that we really did grow to love them. They came to bring us joy.

DAVE: *And then you dropped the bathing pitcher and broke it.*

KORTNEY: *It was an accident.*

It really was an accident, and I thought there'd be no way to glue it back together without her knowing. It was like that episode of *The Brady Bunch* when Bobby and Cindy broke the vase, despite the fact that *Mom always said not to play ball in the house.*

DAVE: *The glue was super obvious.*

KORTNEY: *On* The Brady Bunch?

DAVE: *On my mom's bathing pitcher.*

KORTNEY: *Yes. Which is why I put it up high on a shelf with flowers in it. So she'd never know.*

She would have been devastated if she'd known that we broke it.

DAVE: *Oh, now "we" broke it. Nice.*

She would have been devastated to know it was broken.

DAVE: *She knew.*

KORTNEY: *She did not know.*

DAVE: *She did know. I told her.*

KORTNEY: *YOU TOLD HER?*

DAVE: *I did.*

KORTNEY: *WHY? I put it up high on the shelf with the flowers in it.*

DAVE: *She would have climbed up there to look at it. I had to give her a heads-up.*

KORTNEY: *So she KNOWS about the bathing pitcher?*

DAVE: *Well . . . she knew about the bathing pitcher.*

KORTNEY: *Ugh. I thought she at least died knowing her bathing pitcher was in good hands.*

DAVE: *It is in good hands. And, more important, Butterfingers, it's out of your hands. Up high on the shelf where it can't come to any more harm.*

KORTNEY: *Well, who would have predicted, all those years ago, that your mother's bathing pitcher would get its own chapter in a book?*

DAVE: *My mother would have predicted it. She knew the bathing pitcher had star quality.*

She was right. It does.
Rest in peace, Barb. This one's for you.

DAVE WILSON MASTER CLASS
PUT ON YOUR APRON, AND DO WHAT YOU'VE GOT TO DO

Everyone has a backstory. Some are happy, some are sad, and some leave you covered in question marks, like, *Did that seriously just happen to me?* I like to think my story has a zesty blend of all three and that all of those various twists and turns—the good, the bad, and the ugly—have led me to where I sit today: in my living room, writing a chapter in a book about happy home design, while our geriatric pug, Donnie, waits impatiently for me to give him a bite of my pizza.

People often ask how I went from singer-songwriter to TV house-flipper guy. It's a funny story, really—if you think a grown man crying in a 1971 Volkswagen Beetle is funny. Which, of course, it totally is.

The year was 2001. I had a record deal with Disney, a deal with a renowned music publishing company, and one of the most influential

artist managers in Nashville. Not to mention (okay, I'm going to mention it), I was engaged to the love of my life, my soul mate, Kortney. I was on the top of the world.

Then September 11 happened. And the world stopped turning, as we stared at our television in shock and horror and grieved the loss of people we didn't even know. That day changed America in profound ways—and smaller ways that would reveal themselves later. The ripples of that tragedy shifted the way we live and the way we work, and the music industry was not immune to that shift. Before the year was out, I was called to the offices of Lyric Street Records and asked to leave the label. There was no longer any room in country radio for upbeat, feel-good music from a Canadian artist. The dominoes fell from there. At the end of 2003, I lost my publishing deal, and my manager, too, which made sense, since he had nothing left to manage.

Kortney and I were married by that point, with a baby on the way. I sat behind the wheel of my Volkswagen Beetle for three hours one night, soaking in the fact that everything I had worked so hard for had been erased like it never happened. Other than singing and writing and playing music, I had no skills or valuable work experience. I couldn't *do* anything. But I had to do something. And quickly.

I wrote a résumé—a sad and desperate attempt to make my life experience look useful to strangers—and I hit the streets of downtown Nashville. If there was a Help Wanted sign in the window, I went in. And quickly came back out. It turned out that restaurants and bars were interested only in hiring skilled and experienced workers. *So picky.*

To ease the pain of rejection, I stopped to grab a drink at a family restaurant called Demos', where the manager happened to be filling in as bartender. Like all of the best bartenders, she listened to my tale of woe. *Unlike* all of the best bartenders, she decided to take a risk and offered me a job.

I was ecstatic. This was the sign I needed that everything was going to be okay. I was going to land on my feet. Not only that, I was going to be the best server Nashville had ever seen.

Enthusiasm has always been one of my strong suits.

Predicting my success as a waiter, not so much.

I was abysmal.

In the course of one week, I had managed to make less than two hundred dollars, drop a brown butter spaghetti on a man in a wheelchair, and serve a recovering alcoholic a nonvirgin strawberry daiquiri. There were days when I barely broke even after paying for parking, but when I'd come home late and see my wife and infant child sound asleep, I couldn't bear to tell Kortney the truth. "I made amazing tips tonight!" I'd tell her, so she could rest easy. And then I'd make a mental note of how much more I'd have to earn the next day to turn that white lie into reality.

There were perks to working at Demos', though. And they came in the shape of uneaten chunks of meat. I don't know if you realize this, but people are crazy. They will order a giant steak and eat only *half* of it. Any time I witnessed such blasphemy, I would swoop in, clear the table, and slide that juicy half-steak into my apron. A quick rinse in the bathroom and I'd be eating like a king—if kings ate pilfered meat in bathroom stalls, and who really knows what kings are into.

Some of my happiest times were when customers would leave a roll, so I could make a sandwich.

KORTNEY: *A: That's disgusting. And B: Those were your* happiest *times!?*

DAVE: *Not my happiest times in life. My happiest times as a server.*

While my serving skills improved modestly over time, I knew I needed to supplement my income, so I took any and every opportunity that came my way. Landscaping? *How hard can it be to plant pansies?* Need a DJ? *Just tell me when and where.* I took "fake it till you make it" to the extreme, reporting for duty without a clue in my clue box.

Was it a little humiliating when I was (coincidentally) hired to deejay the party of a peer, celebrating her success at the label I'd been dropped from? It was not a high point of my life, I'll say that. But I survived that too. (Thanks in no small part to the fine gentleman tending bar at that party and his proximity to my DJ station.)

So here I was, a brand-new dad (another role for which I had *zero* preparation), working three jobs (none of which I was particularly good at), and still holding out hope that some day music and I would make our way back to each other. Kortney and I had managed to buy a house at this point, moving into a transitional neighborhood where houses were cheap because most people were still afraid to buy. We were broke, but we owned a home, and we had each other. We also had very old pipes upstairs, which burst over Christmas and flooded the entire house. We came home to two feet of standing water—a very soggy invitation to learn the art of home renovation. Our Realtor friend was so impressed with our work, she suggested we get into flipping houses.

She—like many other people at the time—had had some success doing the same and figured (quite accurately) that I'd be dumb enough to try anything once, if it was legal and promised to pay the bills. It so happened she had a particular little house in mind.

So we took the equity in our house to get a loan, purchased a tiny little house in another part of town for $62,000, and spent the next six weeks fixing it up. The updates were all cosmetic at this point; we were still newbies after all. But we gave the place fresh paint, installed new carpet throughout, put in new windows, and updated fixtures. And then we sold it three weeks later for $135,000.

And the rest is history. We were hooked.

Our real estate agent showed up at Demos' at the end of my shift with the check from the sale, and I quit right there on the spot. I think my manager agreed that this decision was mutually advantageous.

I still have my green apron from that job. I keep it to remind me that hard work will always trump talent or luck alone. Between us, Kortney and I have certainly had our share of both luck and talent. But hard work is what gets us by when times are tough. And hard work is how we pay the universe back when life feels too good to be true.

ADDRESS YOUR
NEED FOR SPEED

———

Think about the times in your life when no one is moving fast enough. For us, it used to be getting out the door for hockey practice. The skates, the sticks, the pads . . . it was like finding and relocating an avalanche three nights a week. We addressed that by dedicating a special corner of the garage to all things hockey. Now (after several years of practice—both hockey practice *and* practicing putting the hockey gear away) no one enters the house until all of the gear is properly stowed. Simple, right?

Putting things in their place sounds so easy, but in practice, it's . . . well, something you have to practice. Over and over and over again, until it becomes routine.

DAVE: *And sometimes she yells.*

KORTNEY: *No, I don't.*

DAVE: *(Yes, she does.)*

KORTNEY: *I encourage and instruct.*

DAVE: *And when that doesn't work . . .*

KORTNEY: *I self-amplify.*

But I try not to yell. Especially in the mornings. When we had three kids, mornings had to be carefully choreographed to get everyone out the door on time. When it worked, it was a beautiful thing that went something like this:

How to Win at Mornings

1. **Plan ahead.** Thirty minutes before bed will save you 40 minutes of morning grief, when everyone's running around and you can't think straight. I'd pack lunches the night before and put backpacks, violin cases, and such by the front door. And for members of the family who tend to become indecisive under morning pressure, consider laying out a nice little outfit the night before.

DAVE: *You don't lay out my little outfits at night.*

KORTNEY: *I was talking about the kids.*

2. **First, you do you.** On weekdays, I pull a page from the flight attendant playbook and secure my own oxygen mask first. Meaning, I don't go downstairs until I'm fully dressed, with makeup and hair done, head on straight, and ready to walk out the door. That way when I'm downstairs, I can focus on what the kids need, and I don't get distracted.

3. **Routine is an art (so frame it).** Meanwhile, each kid has their own checklist with reminders to brush teeth, make bed, put on shoes, etc. Each list is a little different, based on what's age appropriate, and I frame them and hang them on the wall with a note that says "When these things are done, we'll see you at breakfast."

DAVE: *The framed checklists are really helpful. I still use mine.*

4. **Set the routine to music.** Remember when I said our morning routine was carefully choreographed? Well, the best choreography deserves a soundtrack. Setting the morning to music was especially effective when the kids were little . . .

DAVE: *And didn't express strong musical preferences.*

They didn't care what songs we played, but they knew that Song A meant X, Song B meant Y, and when they heard The Jackson 5's "ABC,"

it was time to finish up their cereal and put their dishes in the sink.

DAVE: *And when "Highway to Hell" came on, that was our cue to walk out the door.*

KORTNEY: *Nice.*

The point is, time is valuable. When you respect the clock, it means you respect others and yourself. Unless you're Dave.

DAVE: *The guy who starts every email with "So sorry for the delay . . ."*

KORTNEY: *It makes me crazy.*

DAVE: *I'm sorry. We're not all wired like Kortney Wilson.*

KORTNEY: *Punctuality isn't genetic, Dave. It's a commitment you make and it shows people that you consider their time as valuable as your own.*

DAVE: *I'm sorry, I was late to what you just said. Can you repeat it?*

My mother sets all her clocks ahead 15 minutes, which makes no sense to me. We'll get in the car, and I'll say, "We're late." And she'll say, "No, we're not! The clocks are 15 minutes ahead, so we're actually right on time."

DAVE: *That's awesome! It's like giving yourself a little present every time you look at the clock.*

KORTNEY: *Except that you still know what time it* actually *is. So . . . why not just have the clock set to the correct time?*

DAVE: *So you're saying you hate getting presents.*

KORTNEY: *WHAT?*

DAVE: *Never mind. Can I tell everyone the last step for addressing the need for speed?*

KORTNEY: *Sure. Go for it.*

5. **Waste no time arguing with your wife about whether it's okay to be late.**

KORTNEY: *Thank you. My work here is done.*

FORGO FORMALITY

Rarely used formal living rooms or dining rooms make me crazy—they are such wasted space. If you love hosting frequent four-course dinners for friends, by all means make your dining room a fabulous formal affair. But if that antique table and china cabinet are just collecting dust 364 days a year, it's more than okay to rethink that space altogether and make it useful again. Maybe the dining room becomes a craft room or sewing area. Maybe it will make a great library, or a home office. You don't owe anyone a formal dining room. And if you ever decide to sell your home, you can decide how to address the dining room then. Live to *love* your home. Not to sell it.

Dave and I are pretty casual creatures, and for us, meals and gatherings with friends and family are one of life's great pleasures. Which is why we don't separate our living and dining spaces. They just all flow together. For us, a dining room is a place to break bread and not a place to worry about breaking Grandma's wedding china.

This is a new era. Tradition is no longer the boss of you. If you have fine china and you're worried about it, sell it. And if you love it, *use it*. So what if it chips? Maybe it means you were lucky enough to have eaten a wonderful meal on that china. Make note of it. Make it a memory, not a museum piece.

Don't get me wrong. If displaying something and saving it for posterity brings you joy, by all means do so proudly and prominently. Just don't create opportunities that make you worry. I think that's a pretty good rule all around.

Dave and I don't bring anything into our house if we're not going to use it. For us, nothing is so sacred or precious.

DAVE: *Nothing?*

KORTNEY: *I mean no* thing. *What's sacred and precious to us is family and friendship and the time we spend together.*

DAVE: *And tacos. Oh, and punctuality.*

KORTNEY: *Which, in your case, seems to be a lot less sacred than tacos.*

DAVE: *Okay, you know what? I don't like where this is going. Let's just stick with family and friendship and the time we spend together. (And the time we spend together eating tacos.)*

KORTNEY: *Eating tacos on the chipped china. Sounds good.*

NOT EVERYONE WANTS TO BUY WHAT YOU'RE SELLING

Fact: Someone is going to hate this book and every piece of advice in it. This is perfectly okay. We are each entitled to our opinion, and if you don't find our advice helpful or engaging, I won't hold it against you. I also won't let it change the way I feel about what we've written here. As a wise friend of mine once said, "Not everyone is going to dig your sh*t." And the sooner you can be okay with that, the better.

This is an important life lesson, one that Dave and I started learning long before we began flipping houses or had a television show. And while it hurts sometimes, I've come to believe that every time we experience others' apathy or rejection, it's an opportunity to self-assess and then renew our commitment to what we believe in.

Back when Dave and I were just starting out as a country duo, a friend of ours got us a gig at his corporate holiday party. It was $600 for three hours of singing cover songs to a corporate audience in a sea of cheap wine and cheese plates. This was *big* money to us at the time, and we were determined to do our friend proud.

DAVE: *Thank God he wasn't there.*

KORTNEY: *If he'd been there, maybe his coworkers would have pretended they liked us.*

DAVE: *I didn't want their pity-love.*

KORTNEY: *After that opening song, I would have totally taken their pity-love.*

If our friend had been there to introduce us, maybe the night would have gone differently. The crowd might have been inclined to pay attention. But as it went, Dave and I started our set with no applause or introduction. We were strictly the hired help. On a stage. In a corner. At a corporate party, singing cover songs.

DAVE: *And let's be clear: they weren't even the right cover songs.*

KORTNEY: *How do you know they weren't the right songs? After the first verse, no one was listening.*

DAVE: *Well, that was my first clue that they weren't the right songs.*

The crowd turned to face us when we first started to play, and then it was as if a group decision was being made. *Is this music? Or is this background noise?*

DAVE: *Background noise. It was decided.*

It was like a wave. One person turned away, then another, and another . . . we could have walked offstage right then and no one would have noticed.

DAVE: *But where's the fun in that?*

KORTNEY: *There's no fun in that. We had to own the rejection.*

DAVE: *We more than owned it. We rolled around in it for three hours, like their apathy was a heart-shaped tub filled with hundred-dollar bills.*

By the third song, Dave started rewriting lyrics on the fly. Alison Krauss's "When You Say Nothing at All" became "When No One Listens at All."

DAVE: *Which, of course, didn't matter, because . . .*

KORTNEY: *No one was listening at all.*

I walked offstage in the middle of a song to take a bathroom break, and came back two songs later.

DAVE: *Not a blip on the corporate radar.*

And then we sang that one song—our favorite duet, an original song we wrote called "Explorers"—three times in a row. Just to see if we could.

DAVE: *We could.*

We could have sung that song on repeat for the remainder of the night and no one would have noticed or cared. This crowd was thoroughly, deeply uninterested in the sweet song stylings of Kortney and Dave Wilson.

Dave and I left the event that night feeling a little foolish, not because the crowd didn't like us, but because we'd gone into the night assuming they would. This was a corporate party, where people come for the free food. Or for the camaraderie. Or because it was company policy. They most definitely had not come for the music.

You have to know your audience. It's tempting to think that *if only we're good enough,* we can win everyone's attention and favor. Or, in the case of home design, *if we do everything right,* we can sell the house for top dollar. Or, in the case of *life,* if we're just nice enough, everyone will like us. But it's just not true.

Not everyone wants to buy what you're selling, and no matter how hard you try, you'll never be good enough for everyone. You can only be good enough for you.

Keep doing your thing. Keep singing your song. Keep painting the walls the way you want them.

Listen to advice but don't live by it if it doesn't suit you.

DAVE: *And when you find yourself in a room full of people who couldn't care less about your thing?*

KORTNEY: *Sing your song on repeat.*

DAVE WILSON MASTER CLASS
WARM UP ANY ROOM WITH VINYL

It's been a weekend ritual for years that the first person downstairs in the morning makes breakfast and puts on a record. As convenient as it may be to play Pandora or "ask your smart speaker" to do it for you, Kortney and I agree there's just something about vinyl that sets the mood better than any other media. The sound is warmer, the experience is *slower*. You put on a record and you're committing to settle in for a while. At least until it's time to flip it to the other side. It's kind of like camping—more work, but good for the soul.

Whoever is on vinyl DJ duty has a lot of responsibility. It's up to you to set the tone for the whole day, so you can't screw it up. You have to factor in the season, the weather, overall room temperature, and the events of the night before. It's a science.

If it was a late night with friends and possibly too much wine, you might wake up to some low-key Paul Simon, or, better yet, Air Supply.

Go ahead and laugh, but Air Supply is unquestionably the greatest hangover band of all time. A little "All Out of Love," some Tums, and a couple of aspirin, and you'll be good as new.

And here's the thing about vinyl. Vinyl is cool, regardless of what music you play. (That is the first rule of vinyl.) So you can listen to Air Supply, or Mr. Rogers, or your favorite polka band without sacrificing an ounce of street cred.

Okay. So, let's say Friday was family movie night and everyone fell asleep early and woke up well rested. Boom! Joan Jett, David Bowie, maybe even The Clash. "Should I Stay or Should I Go" + scrambled eggs and bacon = a good day, 99 percent guaranteed.

Kort and I have collected more than 300 records over the years, and the collection is one of the few possessions we would hate to part with. Lennox loves looking at the covers, and we read the lyrics and credits together. Jett and Sully roll their eyes at most of my selections, because they are fools who don't yet understand the transformative power of music, or karma. But one day they'll get it.

When I listen to my favorite record of all time (*Wanna Be a Star* by the band Chilliwack, in case you're curious), I'm transported back in time to when I was a 16-year-old punk from a small town, shooting pucks at the garage door with the music cranked up to 10. Don't even get me started on Def Leppard. You put on *Pyromania* at eight on Saturday morning and watch what happens.

KORTNEY: *Your wife weighs the pros and cons of lighting you on fire?*

Not everyone is sophisticated enough to appreciate Def Leppard. But not everyone moseys out of bed early enough to beat their husband to the turntable either.

Pyromania is the stuff my teenage dreams were made of. I remember thinking that if I just bought a cheap guitar, I could be the next Phil Collen. While I did buy the guitar, surprisingly no one has invited me to join Def Leppard.

Yet.

And that's the beauty of vinyl, folks. It keeps your memories—and sometimes even your dreams—alive. Right there in your living room.

LOVE YOUR PERSON, NOT YOUR PLANS

Dave's was the first face I saw when I moved to Nashville. Head recently shaved for the first time, he greeted my mother and me at the door of Deric Ruttan's house, where a group of committed and talented songwriters were living semi-commune style, working for their big break. Deric was my one connection from Canada, and he'd invited me to stay with him while I found my feet. I remember Dave was wearing a tight pair of corduroy pants that for some reason made me assume he was gay. He welcomed us with a joke and promised my mother he'd take good care of me, which put her immediately at ease. She drove back to Canada and told my dad I'd already met a nice gay man in Nashville who was going to be my friend and look out for me.

I was 19 years old, guns blazing and ready for fame. Dave was eight years older and wiser to the ways of the world.

DAVE: *I was definitely eight years older.*

He'd been pursuing a music career longer than I had. He had experiences and broken dreams under his belt. And his dreams were based in rock and roll, not country music. Nashville was just an affordable pit stop on the way to New York or LA. He wasn't here to meet a girl and get tied down.

DAVE: *But then I met a girl and got tied down. And, to my surprise, I kind of liked it.*

Within a few months of my arrival, Dave and I were living together, much to the chagrin of my parents, who at this point had figured out that Dave was very *not gay*. We were friends and we were in love and we would lie awake late into the night, laughing and listening to music and talking about the future. It was a dream come true for me.

DAVE: *And then every other dream started to come true for you.*

I got my record deal, and a publishing deal, and I was writing twice a day with different songwriters, and hobnobbing and making connections in the music business. Lyric Street

told me I was the Britney Spears of country music. It was only a matter of time, and they were grooming me for fame.

DAVE: *And I was sitting at home trying to remember to groom myself.*

Things were slower to pick up for Dave, and I knew this was hard for him. But in my own ambition and naïveté, I chose to challenge him—rather than be a support. The whirlwind of what seemed like sudden success had gone to my head, and I wasn't as careful with him as I needed to be. I wanted him to embrace Nashville so we could follow this dream together.

Mutual friends thought he was tossing his dreams aside for mine. That he was destined to become Mr. Kortney Kayle (Kortney Kayle was my stage name at the time). And this bothered Dave deeply, and rightfully so.

Still, I didn't see what was coming.

One Saturday morning, he came to me, stone-faced, and said, "We need to talk." Honestly, I was clueless. I thought he was going to say he was being deported. But he was breaking up with me.

"It's not working," he said.

What's not working? I thought. As far as I was concerned, life couldn't be better.

But Dave was panicking.

DAVE: *Because I was in love.*

Nashville was not where he wanted to be. And it was exactly where I wanted to be. There was no way he could follow his dream and stay with me. He had to choose.

He couldn't explain all this to me at the time. Right then he just mumbled man things.

DAVE: *Not working. Dave can't. Dave sorry. Dave and Kortney go bye-bye now. Bye-bye.*

I was devastated. Out of my mind. I had one girlfriend at the time, and I went to her apartment because I didn't know where else to go. She was the only person I knew who was close to my age—and this was, by far, the heaviest thing I'd ever experienced. She tried to talk to Dave on my behalf to find out *what* exactly wasn't working, but he just couldn't articulate it. I sat on her sofa in disbelief.

That night, I went back to our apartment to grab some of my stuff, so I could stay with my girlfriend, but when I walked in, Dave said, "I love you," and I knew I was being given another chance and needed to see our relationship from his perspective. We talked all night. And I started to understand how he might be sacrificing his own dreams by staying with me.

DAVE: *And I started to understand that, even though I had a choice, it wasn't really a choice at all. Music was my first love, but it had nothing on this one.*

The next morning, we went for coffee at a little shop called Bongo Java, and to my enormous joy and relief, Dave said to me, "I will never leave you. You mark my words. I will never leave you."

KORTNEY: *And I believed you.*

DAVE: *I believed me too. But I didn't see it as giving up on my dream anymore. I saw it as being handed a different dream. One that was a hell of a lot prettier than the first one.*

In that moment, I was still too starry-eyed to imagine that maybe neither of our dreams would go quite as we had planned. But I knew that, whatever happened, we were going to be happy, and we were going to be happy together.

SAY YES

Before Dave and I were engaged, I was supplementing my songwriting by working part time as a photographer's assistant. It was not glamorous work by any stretch, but I needed money to fund my demo tapes, and I welcomed the opportunity to do something in the entertainment business, even if only peripherally. The photographer I worked for specialized in product photography, and his biggest client at the time was a major tire manufacturer. My job was to pick the hundreds of tiny rubber nubs (the technical term for these is "vent spews") off the tire treads before he snapped each shot. This was before the days of easy digital retouching, so there was no "vent spew removal tool" he could use to fix the photos in postproduction. It was all on me. And I had the blisters to prove it. It was not exactly what I'd expected to find myself doing in Nashville, but if I was going to do it, I was going to do it right. And if that didn't teach me to sweat the details, nothing would.

One afternoon my boss mentioned that he'd gotten an assignment to shoot a print ad for a chocolate company, and he needed a young woman to model. The pay was $600 for a day's work; would I be interested? *Hell YES, I was interested.* Six hundred dollars to pose with a chocolate bar? I posed with chocolate bars at home all the time for free. This was amazing. Before I could get home to tell Dave, my boss called to tell me one more detail. There would be another model on the shoot—a young guy— playing my love interest. He wanted to make sure I was comfortable with that.

I was so excited about the $600, I would have kissed an alpaca on the lips if that's what the job required, but I ran it all by Dave just in case. "Yes!" he said. "Of course you have to do it." He congratulated me—and then congratulated *us* for getting ahead of next month's rent.

About a week before the shoot, the photographer called to tell me the other model had canceled. Would Dave be interested in subbing for him? "Does the client know Dave's bald?" I asked. I wasn't sure if that was the aesthetic they were going for. He assured me that the scene called for a guy wearing a hat, shot from behind. Basically if Dave was willing, he was hired.

Of course Dave was willing. And in this case, he was *more* than willing. Now we were *both* getting paid $600. We were going to be rich!

On the day of the shoot, I arrived on set first, and there, under the lights, was the most gorgeous chocolate-brown vintage Volkswagen Beetle convertible. Our love of the Bug is one of

I did as I was told, and inside the box, I found a gorgeous diamond ring. Dave looked at me, paused for a moment, and said, "Will you marry me?"

Everyone on set went wild. Assistants brought in bouquets of red roses. And even better—the photographer was capturing the whole moment on camera.

"All of this is for you," Dave said.

I was stunned. Looking at the lights and the set and the car and the crew, I started to comprehend that Dave had orchestrated this entire shoot so he could surprise me in this beautiful, unforgettable way.

After I caught my breath, I joked, "So we're not getting paid $1,200?"

"No," Dave said. "But you get to keep the car."

Here I was, sitting in the car of my dreams, with the man of my dreams, having just received a proposal I couldn't have cooked up in my *wildest dreams*. Paycheck or not, I had never felt richer.

Everything you need to know about Dave Wilson can be summarized by that proposal. He is a true romantic. Creative and clever and funny and generous. He is always up for an adventure and can charm just about anyone into becoming his partner in crime. Most of all, he goes to extraordinary lengths to make this one life of ours absolutely unforgettable. Hands down, Dave Wilson is the best thing I've ever said yes to, because he doesn't just *say* yes—he lives it—by being all in, all the time, and inspiring me to do the same.

many things Dave and I have in common, and I called him immediately. "You won't believe the car we're shooting in," I said. "It's GORGEOUS. You're going to have to brace yourself."

We started shooting, and Dave and I were yukking it up playing lovebirds in the Beetle's front seat. After a few minutes, the director told us he wanted to try shooting with the top down. He instructed me to reach into the glove compartment and pop the top. I opened the glove compartment and looked around for the right button. There was nothing in there but a tiny box. The room went silent.

"Open it," the director said.

I was completely confused, thinking he was still talking about the convertible roof. "How do I open it?"

"The box," he said. "Open the box."

STAY PLAYFUL

———

Dave is our family's funny bone. If I run a tight ship, Dave runs the ship's comedy club.

DAVE: *Which is located on the poop deck, by the way.*

KORTNEY: *Of course it is.*

If it weren't for Dave, I'd likely let April Fools' Day pass without pranking the kids, the tooth fairy would have far less personality, and Bobby, our Elf on the Shelf, would have met an "untimely" death shortly after Thanksgiving.

DAVE: *You can't kill an Elf on the Shelf. They're made of magic.*

KORTNEY: *Magic and polyester. Which is highly flammable.*

DAVE: *You are a sick woman.*

KORTNEY: *I'll tell you who's a sick woman. The woman who ups her elf-on-the-shelf game every year, until Mr. Sprinkles, wearing a bespoke chef's uniform, is in the kitchen and making crepes for a family of six.*

DAVE: *Did that actually happen?*

KORTNEY: *Probably!*

The Elf on the Shelf really chaps my—

DAVE: *This is a family book, Kortney.*

And that's why I have Dave. Dave can do the Elf on the Shelf. When my last shred of holiday patience has been pecked out by three French hens, he's standing by the blender, crafting another brilliant—and usually rhyming—letter from Bobby the Elf.

Would it be easier to phone it in or forgo elves on shelves altogether? YES. But there's magic in these moments, and not just for the kids. When I see Dave giving the elf his all, it reminds me how much more satisfying—and, let's face it, fun—it is to do life joyfully.

Bobby made a super mess
I was hungry I confers.
Just trying to get my sugar fix
but wast'int happy with this mix
Let me give you the whole scoop
Bobby likes those fruite Loops ~~Loops~~
If you get those, it would be rad
without them Bobby gets reel mad.
Well that is all I need to say
Have yourself A super DAY!!!

Love
Bobby

IDENTIFY YOUR DROP SPOT

An important part of loving your home is being able to leave it. This poses a bit of a challenge when you (and by "you," I mean "Dave") are forever misplacing your keys, wallet, phone, wallet, sunglasses, and did I say "wallet" already? If I had a dollar for every time we had to cancel our credit cards because Dave's wallet went missing, we wouldn't even need credit cards.

> **DAVE:** *Okay, that might be a bit of an exaggeration. But I'm going to forgive it because I love that Southernism you threw in there about how my wallet just "went missing."*

> **KORTNEY:** *Yes, this is one of the great benefits of living in the South: we don't lose things here, they "go missing."*

> **DAVE:** *I love this. The burden of guilt is on the object itself. The darn wallet went missing and there wasn't a thing I could do to stop it. Wallets can be incredibly willful.*

If your wallet has a mind of its own, like Dave's, and just won't listen to reason, this may not help you at all. But for the rest of us, I can't emphasize this tip enough: you've *got* to have a drop spot. It can be a basket, a console table, a chest of drawers, or a hanging shelf—whatever works in your space (and whatever you're least likely to ignore). Put it immediately inside your main entrance (or whatever entrance you mainly use), and before you step one foot further into the house, you unload. Your keys, your phone, your sunglasses, *your wallet*, and whatever else you need to leave the house in a timely fashion. Eventually this routine will become second nature, and you will speed up your exit strategy by *at least* 50 percent.*

> *****DAVE:** *Results may vary, depending on who you marry.*

STOW THOSE SHOES

———

Growing up in Canada, I was accustomed to taking off my shoes when I entered someone's home (including my own), but since moving to the United States, I've adapted to local custom. It's not universal by any means. There are still plenty of Americans whose claws come out when the shoes *don't* come off, but for the most part, I've found it's pretty common here for outdoor shoes to be worn inside the home.

Whatever your preference—shoes on or shoes off—I'm willing to bet that when the shoes *do* come off, they don't always march themselves upstairs and into the closet where they belong.

DAVE: *No, our shoes prefer to loiter in the middle of the hallway, catching up with old friends. They're extremely social.*

As much as I *hate* to break up the party, shoes belong in one of two places: on your feet or out of sight. And by "out of sight," I do not mean "tossed willy-nilly in a hall closet to canoodle in a stinky, tangled-up mess."

DAVE: *Are we still talking about shoes, or did we switch to teenagers?*

KORTNEY: *Teenagers canoodling in closets is a whole other tip.*

DAVE: *Right. Ten out of 10 parents do not recommend.*

If you elect to store your shoes in a communal closet, be sure to carve out a space in the closet that's shoe-specific. Without a designated space for every item, closets will start breeding clutter the minute you close the door.

In walk-in closets, suspended shelving keeps shoes up off the floor and organized. If your closet runs small, an over-the-door shoe organizer will serve the same purpose. But first, you need to draw a line in the sand about how many pairs of shoes you're willing to entertain in the common area.

Our rule is one pair per person. And this is the only time I break my "out of sight" rule. Each Wilson is allowed to keep one pair of shoes by the front door—for easy access.

DAVE: *"For easy policing" is more like it.*

My favorite options include crates, cubbies, bags, and baskets. Here's how to figure out which style suits you best.

Shoe Storage Styles

Low-key rustic. A little dirt never hurt anyone. Your home is about personality, not perfection. Maybe you live in a cold-weather zone, where boots are worn six months of the year. Old crates can be configured into shelving for shoes of different sizes. And they're inexpensive, so you won't be upset if the crates get dirty or scuffed.

Summer vibes. Warm-weather shoes like flats and flip-flops are a great fit for the shoe bags that hang on the back side of a door. Keep one in the mudroom for easy access (and eye-level reminding).

Sweet and practical. Cubbies are cute, but if you have a wall that's wide open, consider adding shoe hooks. For reasons that require further study, I've found that little kids are far more likely to hang up their shoes than they are to store them.

I'd like to live in a catalog, please. Baskets are our go-to shoe-storage solution at Wilson Central. Each family member gets a labeled basket to store shoes under the console table (remember our drop spot?) by the front door. If you can't slip the basket back under because it's overflowing with shoes, go directly to your room, do not pass go, and do not collect $200. Put. Your. Shoes. Away.

REMEMBER THE RULE OF THREE

Three is a powerful number. Photographers use the rule of thirds to compose their shots, marketers and speakers use lists of three to make their messages more memorable, and designers use groupings of three in staging all the time. Once you tune in to the power of threes, you'll begin to notice it everywhere—and you'll want to put it to work in your home as well.

When in Doubt, Group Items in Threes

Books, accessories, artwork, and even furniture pieces look best in groups of three. Notice how one item looks lonely, two objects seem stagnant, but three pieces grouped together somehow feel *just right*. Our eyes are drawn to odd numbers of things, in part because they register as a pattern, which makes the grouping feel more intentional. If you want to break the rule of threes, that's okay, but group in odd numbers, never even. Five and seven can work just as well—and nine, well, it's just three groups of three, which makes it great for gallery walls where you want more volume without sacrificing balance.

You Can Even Use the Rule of Three with Color

It's not a hard-and-fast rule, but a great guideline for choosing and distributing color throughout a space. Choose one main color—your hero color—to make up 60 percent of the room, a secondary color (like an accent wall or bold sofa color and some art) to make up 30 percent of the room, and a third accent color to make up the remaining 10 percent. The room will feel balanced, cohesive, and colorful.

DAVE: *I see what you did there. Balanced. Cohesive. And Colorful. That's three things.*

KORTNEY: *It's like magic.*

BUY ART YOU LOVE

—

I am by no means an expert on art. And frankly, I'm not in a financial position to cultivate that expertise. The art I'm inclined to fall in love with—big, bold contemporary art—is expensive enough when it is quietly hanging in a gallery. As soon as someone with industry credentials declares it worthy of praise, the price tag will for sure be hanging squarely out of my reach.

So while I don't consider myself a collector or connoisseur, I do know what I like, and I think I have a pretty good eye for what will work well in a given space. When it comes to my own home, though, the art has to have more than size, style, and color going for it. I really have to love it to live with it.

The major pieces of art we've purchased for our home have been love-at-first-sight experiences. Every time. The painting that hangs in the foyer over the landing of our staircase hit me like Cupid's arrow when I saw it for the first time. Dave and I were walking through an arts and crafts fair on the Saturday before Mother's Day one year, and I stopped in my tracks. "I love it," I said.

DAVE: *It's a typewriter.*

I looked at the price tag and quickly *stopped stopping in my tracks. Pretend you didn't see that, Kortney. Pretend it's just a typewriter.*

DAVE: *It is just a typewriter.*

KORTNEY: *It's symbolic of the convergence of old and new. Its scale and prominence in the frame speaks to the enormous potential energy of words that have yet to be written. It's so much more than a typewriter, Dave.*

DAVE: *That's so weird. It totally looks like a typewriter to me.*

But as far as I was concerned, we couldn't afford it. And I can't afford to dwell on things I can't afford, so we left the fair empty-handed that afternoon. Little did I know, Dave's mental gears were already turning.

DAVE: *Long story short: I snuck back out and bought her the typewriter.*

KORTNEY: *And then I was mysteriously called across the street to consult the neighbor on a design emergency.*

DAVE: *I had to get the painting in the house without you seeing me.*

KORTNEY: *So you picked the one neighbor who has ZERO sense of urgency when it comes to design. And there she was trying to pretend to panic about whether or not to center her dining room table. I knew something was up. But I had no idea what.*

DAVE: *So you were surprised? I won?*

KORTNEY: *Actually, I'd say I won. I love this piece more with every passing year.*

And that's the sign of a great find. It never gets old. So my advice, if you're in the market for a new piece of art, is to ramp up your shopping *right* before Mother's Day or some other special occasion and make sure your significant other is a sneaky romantic who's along for the ride. In all seriousness, though, art should be an emotional purchase. If it speaks to you strongly and you can afford to listen (or maybe even if you can't), snap it up and never look back. You won't be sorry.

HANG A GALLERY WALL THE EASY WAY

Mixing and matching art and photos of different styles allows you to get big-art impact with *little* art pieces. A gallery wall is also a great way to kick off conversation when guests come to visit. In our house, we have a gallery wall that consists of funny family photos, art made by friends, old magazine covers, and more. The frames are a mix of colors and styles, but the gallery all comes together beautifully, thanks to this handy layout tip.

A Step-by-Step Guide to Hanging a Gallery Wall

1. Measure the wall area where you plan to hang your gallery wall, so you know how much space you have to work with.

2. Lay all of your art on the *floor*, within those measurements, and reconfigure the pieces until you're happy with the way they look together. Trust your instincts here. If the grouping feels unbalanced, try redistributing the colors and textures of your pictures and frames until it all looks like one cohesive unit.

3. Trace each frame (or piece, if you're hanging unframed elements) on an individual piece of kraft paper, cut it out, and mark on the cutout where the nail should go.

4. Tape all of your paper elements to the wall in the same configuration you've laid out on the floor.

5. Take a step back. Is it framing the sofa or console table the way you'd imagined? Is it too wide—or is the spacing just right? Adjust the configuration on the wall (and do the same on the floor) until you're satisfied.

6. Remember the dots you marked earlier? Those are where you're going to put your nails. Tap them right through the papers, then remove the papers when you're done.

7. I like to hang each piece as I go, to slowly reveal my finished (and perfectly spaced) gallery wall.

Notice I didn't tell you *how* to arrange your gallery wall. That's because there are so many ways to do it—and none of them is wrong.

Options for Hanging a Gallery Wall

Abstract mix. If your tastes are eclectic, like mine, mix up the colors and sizes and textures of your frames and arrange them in an abstract shape on the wall. No firm border necessary.

Modern master. If tight corners and straight edges are more your style, try a grid formation, pairing pieces of equal size and consistent style.

Black and white. A black-and-white gallery wall will never go out of style, but you might consider spicing it up by having one black frame hold a bold color print, preferably one right in the middle.

Monochromatic. Choose one dominant color, like a Prussian blue, to make your gallery wall an exciting focal point. You can vary the artwork, from black-and-white photos to paintings and prints in which blue is the dominant hue.

Pretty pastels. Light wood and white frames around pretty pastel prints add interest to a room without being overwhelming. I love a sweet mix of florals and dreamscapes and typography assembled over a console table filled with living greens.

Whatever your gallery style, go for it with gusto—and don't let perfection be the enemy of awesome.

MAKE WAY FOR THE LAST MINUTE

———

I've always been a planner. I despise chaos and clutter. And I am nothing if not organized. So it surprises some people to learn that my favorite kind of party to throw is the one that's thrown together at the last minute. Totally unplanned. Totally impromptu. And, if weather permits, we head *outdoors* on our big front porch, where we can welcome a few strangers into the mix. I'm serious when I tell you that few things bring me more joy than rounding up friends and their families (and whatever we have in our collective pantries) for some improvised food and entertainment.

You know, now that I think about it, maybe this is *why* I run such a tight ship all the time: so I'm ready for the fun when it's ready for me. No two days in our lives are the same right now. Calendars are constantly shifting. Once you lock in the big events that can't budge, it can feel like a chore to carve out casual time with friends. Even a master multitasker like me can't convince all of the stars to align when I want them to. What I've learned, though, is that I can be prepared with an open door and an open heart when the stars happen to align on their own.

We keep the porch prepped and the pantry stocked for those late afternoons when you see friends out walking and say, "Hey, what are you guys doing tonight? No plans? Come over!"

DAVE: *And somehow those two people always turn into 20. What kind of dark magic is that?*

KORTNEY: *I pick up my phone and repeat "Hey, what are you guys doing tonight?" to several different people, and then they bring their kids.*

DAVE: *Oh. Well, that sucks the mystery right out of it.*

There is something magical about a last-minute gathering, though. Everyone's relaxed, there are no expectations; we're all just in the moment.

One of my all-time favorite examples of this happened a few summers ago. It was a lazy Saturday (for the kids, anyway), and the boys across the street had recruited our kids and some others to perform an abridged version of the musical *Les Misérables* on their front porch. They raided our closets for costumes and spent the better part of the afternoon (unbeknownst to us) going door to door *selling* tickets to their show.

DAVE: *How much were the tickets?*

KORTNEY: *I think they were $5 for the front row. $1 for the cheap seats.*

DAVE: *That explains all the empty chairs waiting for us in the front row.*

Around five o'clock, the kids came clamoring for us to "take our seats," and Dave and I crossed the street to find a small crowd of ticket holders standing in our neighbor's yard, waiting for the show to begin. We didn't know half of these people. And neither did the parents of the boy who spearheaded this production. They just walked out their front door to a yard full of strangers.

DAVE: *And to their son Gus, wearing his mom's dress and ankle boots.*

KORTNEY: *He wasn't Gus in that moment. He was Fantine.*

DAVE: *That was one of the most moving renditions of "I Dreamed a Dream" I've ever heard.*

Long story short (and believe me, even the abridged version of *Les Misérables* is not a short story): when the show was over, all of the adults were cracking up and chatting and introducing themselves.

DAVE: *And your party-time sensor started beeping so loudly, I immediately had to call and order six pizzas.*

KORTNEY: *It had to happen. You can't go see a show and not have a slice of pizza afterward.*

So yes, not only did this afternoon of spontaneous theater lead to an impromptu party back at our house, it was the beginning of an amazing friendship with neighbors we had never met, who took a chance and bought tickets to a kid's porch theater production. They remain our close friends to this day.

KORTNEY: *So many of the best things in my life have happened when I stopped overthinking and decided to just go with the flow.*

DAVE: *The flow knows.*

KORTNEY: *The flow does know.*

FIND YOUR FOCAL POINT

———

What's the first thing you notice when you walk into a room? What are your eyes immediately drawn to? It might be a gorgeous piece of art, or a fabulous chandelier. Maybe it's a console table with a large bouquet of lilies (my favorite). Maybe it's a sweeping staircase, or a cozy fireplace, or a sweet velvet settee. Or maybe it's a giant mountain of mismatched shoes tangled up like a pile of spaghetti.

For better or for worse, the thing that draws your eye and commands your attention *is* your focal point, and it speaks volumes about your aesthetic and lifestyle.

A strong focal point not only sets the mood of the room, it can distract from a home's less flattering features. If, say, the floors are a bit warped or uneven, you can draw the eye upward. If the walls are flat and neutral, you can add texture. You're the director. This is your stage. Have fun with it.

I love to create focal points that involve texture, and it's a theme you'll see repeated throughout our house. An exposed brick fireplace in the foyer. An accent wall made of reclaimed barnwood in the kitchen. Repeating the theme gives the home a feeling of continuity, while limiting the texture to the focal point of each room keeps it from becoming monotonous or overbearing. Remember, it's all about balance.

How to Create a Focal Point

Start with the obvious. What's the biggest thing in the room? A giant picture window? A grand staircase? A stunning fireplace? A vaulted ceiling? We're naturally drawn to epic scale, so if your room has one of these features, play it up and let the rest of the room play a supporting role. If you're lucky enough to have two or more such areas in a room, just choose

one to punch up, so they're not competing for attention.

Create contrast. Texture is one way to create contrast. Color is another. If your decor is neutral, a bold painting, accent wall, or piece of furniture is going to command attention. If your decor is monochromatic, you can get the same effect by contrasting color values (light against dark, or vice versa).

Isolate an element. It's tempting when designing a space to put pretty things everywhere the eye can see. But when you isolate one element, you're basically shining a spotlight on it, accentuating its beauty or uniqueness. This technique is often used in minimalist spaces; think of a painting on an otherwise blank wall, or a sculpture centered at the edge of a modern patio.

When in doubt, an oversize chandelier or a large mirror over a fireplace mantel are classic focal points that work every time.

GO WITH THE FLOW

—

Real estate agents are always talking about homes having "great flow," but what does that really mean in practice?

DAVE: *To me, the working definition of "good flow" is that you can easily use your downstairs to reenact Tom Cruise's iconic dance scene from* Risky Business *without knocking your shins or bruising your man hips on an oversize buffet or coffee table.*

KORTNEY: *Wow. That was really . . . specific.*

DAVE: *Thank you.*

With open and semi-open floor plans growing in popularity, many of the houses I show have terrific flow when they're lightly staged, or completely unfurnished. Then humans move in with their oversize sectionals and massive farm tables and suddenly these houses feel—

DAVE: *Constipated? Like they've been eating nothing but highly processed cheese.*

KORTNEY: *Again. That was . . . alarmingly specific.*

DAVE: *I'm a storyteller by nature.*

The Cornerstones of Great Flow

Clearly established traffic patterns. The path through a room should be immediately obvious and free of obstacles. If people have to bob and weave to get from one room to the next, you have a flow problem. Rearrange the furniture to establish a clear path from point A to point B.

Room to move. If you have to angle your body a certain way to squeeze past a piece of furniture, or you find yourself perpetually stubbing your toe or bruising your hip on *that same damn*

sofa chair, I hate to break it to you, but it's time to rightsize your furnishings. No matter how much you love that farm table, if your guests can't push their chairs out without scraping the walls, it's just not working. The smaller the space you're trying to furnish, the more difficult it can be to maintain good flow. Replacing sharp corners with round edges (for example, a round coffee table instead of a square one) is a quick fix that works wonders.

A guide for the eye. Varying heights, colors, textures, and finishes creates visual interest and draws attention to different areas of the room. At the same time, repetition of colors, shapes, and elements creates *flow*—so the eye senses a connection between these elements and moves naturally and rhythmically through the space.

MAKE ART WITH PEOPLE YOU LOVE

Dave and I have an eclectic collection of art, with all different colors, styles, mediums, and price points in the mix. While each piece has some significance or story behind it, my favorites are the ones that make me smile or laugh out loud every time I look at them, because the memories they hold are far more valuable than the pieces themselves.

So how did I get my hands on these masterpieces?

DAVE: *With bribes, of course!*

KORTNEY: *Not bribes. Just pizza and wine and good friends.*

DAVE: *Good friends who you bribed with pizza and wine so they'd come to your house and paint you a picture.*

I call it "having a party with food at it." Dave calls it "bribery."

DAVE: *I guess that says something about my self-esteem.*

KORTNEY: *Ya think?*

Whatever you call it, inviting friends over to collaborate on a piece of art is always an epic adventure, and I've never *not* loved the end result.

I start with a giant canvas, the bigger the better, and lay it out on the back deck over a giant sheet of painter's plastic. I provide a variety of paint colors and brushes of all shapes and sizes. Then I lay down the ground rule: no one leaves the party without contributing to the canvas. I don't care if it's a line or a dot or a toe print, but everyone *must* leave their mark. And at the end of the night, we have an interesting work of art and more than enough memories to go with it.

If the collaborative approach doesn't appeal to you, you can take a more solitary approach. We do this with family over the holidays, as a fun substitute for the "Dirty Santa" or "White Elephant" gift exchange. Instead of everyone getting a gift, they get a canvas and some paint. And a two-hour time limit. Each artwork gets a number, and at the end of the night, we hold a lottery to determine which piece goes home

with whom. To sweeten the deal (or sour it, depending on whose painting you end up with), every participant must display their "prize" in a prominent spot for one year.

Of course, the art's not the sole point of these parties. It's really just the focal point, an anchor for our memories. Some of my friends are visual artists, but most are not. And something magical happens when we connect outside of our comfort zone, tasked with *making* something, in addition to memories.

COUNT YOUR CHICKENS

———

A few years ago, as a reward for surviving season one of *Masters of Flip,* we took the family to Malibu for two weeks. Friends of ours generously offered up their house by the beach, and we fell in love with the breathtaking scenery and laid-back lifestyle. We also fell in love with their chickens.

Right outside the master bedroom was a coop with six or seven chickens. They appeared to be in constant conversation with one another, squawking and tittering like stars of their own reality show. In no time, these quirky birds strutted straight into our hearts. We'd play rock-paper-scissors to decide who got to get the eggs each day, and we quickly found out that each of us had been sneaking the chickens extra dried worms (a chicken delicacy) without the others knowing. We were smitten, and I, being a vegetarian, was firmly back on the egg train, having tasted these amazing, fresh organic eggs.

Flash forward 18 months, to Christmas morning, and the kids were about to come unglued from excitement—even more so than usual for a Christmas morning. I couldn't figure out what all the fuss was about. Dave and I don't typically exchange gifts (though he does write me a song every year), so I wasn't expecting any surprises, and then he told me to go outside to get my gift.

DAVE: *Did you think it was a car?*

KORTNEY: *I kind of did. Which would have been crazy. So I'm glad it wasn't.*

The kids led me outside, and when I opened my eyes, there was a giant chicken coop with a big red bow around it. I was completely shocked.

DAVE: *Like, good shocked?*

KORTNEY: *More like "Oh my god, we have a giant chicken coop in our backyard and we've never even talked about it" shocked.*

DAVE: *Kind of like when I surprised you with a geriatric pug for Mother's Day?*

KORTNEY: *Very similar. But at least the chickens don't have to wear a diaper.*

There was no going back, of course. Dave had worked so hard designing this coop, and the kids were *so* excited. I had no choice but to roll with it. And I'm really glad I did. We have four chickens, and they each lay about an egg per day. The eggs are so good we fight over

them. And if the chickens are having a slow spell, it's first come, first served.

Obviously, I'm not suggesting that everyone go out and get chickens. They are definitely not what you'd call a "home essential." But if the idea appeals to you, I can tell you our little ladies have given us a great deal of joy.

A Few Words of Caution

- Not all municipalities allow livestock, so you need to do your research. Where we live, we're allowed four chickens and no roosters. (And no, you do not need a rooster to get eggs. That's not how that works.)

- They're not the most *even-tempered* birds, and they will occasionally peck each other

to death. What starts out as a means of communication can quickly escalate into full-blown assault.

- Chickens are also extremely territorial, so if you lose one (because, say, it's been pecked to death), you can't just add another to the coop. You have to introduce the birds slowly, under supervision, until they can get to know each other.

DAVE: *At some point, you stop and ask yourself why you have chickens speed-dating in your garage. Are the eggs that good?*

KORTNEY: *The eggs are really good, but . . . yeah. I see your point.*

DAVE: *You know, it wasn't actually the speed dating that had me questioning our sanity. It was when that one chicken died of a yeast infection. I was like, do I really need this?*

KORTNEY: *Yeah, death by yeast infection is not a good way for any woman to go.*

- Chickens are fairly easy to maintain, but you do need to close their coop at night to protect them from predators. This can pose a problem if you travel a lot.

- And if you do let your ladies (or gents) out to roam the yard, it's adorable, but do that for only a few minutes. If you leave them too long, they'll make a huge mess and peck every inch of your grass until there's nothing left.

DAVE: *And their chicken feed is expensive. So if you're getting chickens to save money on eggs, don't bother. When we did the math, I think each of our eggs costs about $17.50.*

KORTNEY: *Yeah, this is turning out to be a really terrible "tip." I'm not even sure what we're advising here.*

DAVE: *I think we may be advising ourselves to get rid of the chickens?*

KORTNEY: *No! Nothing that extreme. I love the chickens. They're totally impractical, but they make me happy. That's kind of the point here. Not everything has to make sense. If, for example, after hearing everything we've said about chickens, you still want chickens . . . you've got to honor the impulse. That's what keeps life interesting.*

DAVE: *And if you're still on the fence about having your own coop, you shouldn't feel bad if you chicken out.*

KORTNEY: *Ba-dum-ch.*

DAVE: *[Cymbal]*

DAVE WILSON MASTER CLASS
THROW THE BALL

———

Something happens when you play catch with your kid. The easy back-and-forth, the unforced conversation. You get into a rhythm, and it's like magic. That's why no matter what I'm doing, no matter how busy I am, no matter how rotten or mouthy they were being just hours before, if one of my kids asks me to go outside and throw the ball with them, I'm going to go outside and throw the ball. The ball throw is one of the great privileges of parenting, and it has a limited shelf life. The day will come, way too soon, maybe even next week, when no one wants to throw the ball anymore, so I'm going to catch these moments—every darn one of them—while I can.

UNPLUG TO RECHARGE

On Father's Day last year, the kids planned a bunch of activities for the family. When Dave came home, Sully was at the door with a box he'd decorated that said "Deposit All Phones Here." I wanted to cry. As much as our kids love technology, they've also come to crave a different kind of connection because of it. Dave and I can too often be found face-first in our screens. The nature of our work requires us to be accessible to a lot of people, at unpredictable hours, and it can feel like an endless cycle of answering questions, recalibrating schedules, buying, selling, flipping, filming, planning, and promoting. We love it, and wouldn't trade it for anything—but from time to time, we have to remind ourselves to shut it all down.

> **DAVE:** *Or the kids have to remind us.*

> **KORTNEY:** *Which we want to avoid.*

So, in addition to our ongoing effort to *put down our phones and look each other in the eye,* we've also instituted some more formal phone-free family traditions that all of us look forward to.

PAJAMA DAYS

Each year on January 1, we put a bunch of dates (all weekdays) into a jar and draw one. Come hell or high water, on that day, we will all stay home from school or work, stay in our pj's, and watch movies, bake brownies, and play board games all day, as a family, phone-free.

EVERYONE PICK ONE

I imagine few households will reach consensus about what makes the "perfect" family activity, so why not let everyone pick one? We did this over the holiday break and it was so much fun.

> **DAVE:** *Four out of five would agree.*

> **KORTNEY:** *Yeah, your hot chocolate walk was kind of a bust.*

> **DAVE:** *Granted, it was minus seven hundred degrees out, which didn't help.*

> **KORTNEY:** *There's nothing like your teeth chattering to the CLACK, CLACK, CLACK of Jett dribbling a street hockey puck while you're trying to enjoy a pleasant family stroll.*

DAVE: *And then when we asked him to run the hockey stick back home, so we could hear ourselves think . . .*

KORTNEY: *HE WALKED. AS. SLOWLY. AS HE POSSIBLY. COULD.*

DAVE: *Like a teenage snail. In a hoodie.*

KORTNEY: *While we stood on the corner, waiting. And waiting. And our circulatory systems started to shut down.*

DAVE: *And then we all died and were dead.*

KORTNEY: *YES! FAMILY TIME IS THE BEST.*

So, fair enough. It won't always look like a commercial for Swiss Miss. But you've still got to do it.

DAVE: *Do it for the dance party.*

KORTNEY: *That was my idea. It was a good one, right?*

We all danced (and I'll admit, I did take the phone out to get a picture). Then Sully chose a board game, which we all played, and Sully won.

DAVE: *Total coincidence.*

And Lennox chose coloring while watching a movie, which yielded some very nuanced artwork.

DAVE: *I do love coloring.*

KORTNEY: *And you're very good at it.*

The point is—love it or not—everyone has to participate in everyone else's activity.

DAVE: *And if you're smart, you'll schedule the eldest child's activity at the end.*

True, teens can be a bit fickle when it comes to participation, so they might need a little extra incentive to keep their head in the game. A family game of street hockey (Jett's choice) was just the ticket. And a perfect ending to an *almost* perfect day.

TOURISTS IN YOUR OWN TOWN

I know a lot of families who make it a point to paint the town as tourists in their own cities, and for good reason. It's a lot of fun! Especially in a city like Nashville, where the downtown district is a mecca for country music enthusiasts. The streets are lined with honky-tonks and souvenir shops, and no shortage of live music and entertainment.

DAVE: *And karaoke.*

KORTNEY: *Yes. Lots of karaoke, which may not always qualify as music, but usually makes for great entertainment.*

DAVE: *Do you remember that guy in the neon chaps singing Reba McEntire's "Fancy"?*

KORTNEY: *I'm not sure I want to remember that.*

DAVE: *He was amazing. He had glitter in his beard.*

KORTNEY: *Could he sing?*

DAVE: *I don't know. I could barely hear him over the neon chaps and beard glitter.*

No doubt Nashville is a colorful city with lots to see and do, but you really have to slow down and look up to see it the way a newcomer would see it for the first time. It's a brain shift, but toggling over to tourist mode seriously makes you feel like you're on vacation.

DAVE: *It also makes your wallet feel like it's on vacation.*

KORTNEY: *As in "your wallet gets a break"?*

DAVE: *As in "my wallet is about to spontaneously combust from overexertion like it does every time we go on vacation."*

KORTNEY: *I know. I wonder how our kids made it this far in their Nashville lives without fringe vests and cowboy hats.*

DAVE: *And cowboy-boot key chains . . . and sunglasses shaped like the Nashville skyline.*

KORTNEY: *Admit it. Buying souvenirs is part of the fun of being a tourist in your own town. When in Rome, right?*

DAVE: *When in Rome, you don't have to buy ALL of the pope bobbleheads.*

KORTNEY: *If pope bobbleheads are a thing, I may need to buy all of them.*

Bobbleheads or no bobbleheads, try the tourist route on for size. And don't forget to take some photos of your "family vacation."

DAVE WILSON MASTER CLASS
THERE IS ONLY ONE ROAD-TRIP RULE

———

We live in the age of the Global Positioning System. It's an amazing time to be alive! We can punch our destination into a little computer, and the computer will tell us exactly how long it will take us to get there. Therefore, there is no longer any excuse what-so-freakin'-ever for kids of time-telling age to ask their parents, "Are we there yet?"

Hell no, we're not there yet.

Do you know how I know we're not there yet (other than the fact that we are clearly *here* in a still-very-much-moving vehicle)?

GPS, baby!

"There" is exactly 148.7 miles away, and no one in this car will be experiencing the feeling of "there" until 4:37 Eastern Standard Time, so put a sock in it.

IT'S OKAY TO GO GRAY

Because there are so many grays to choose from, this go-to color isn't going anywhere any time soon. Inside or out, a good gray blends beautifully with *everything*—from jewel tones and metallics to pastels and other neutrals. One thing to be aware of with gray interior walls: blue grays, while beautiful, don't play as nicely with other colors as their more neutral counterparts and should be treated as the dominant color in the space, as opposed to a neutral backdrop.

MAKE MEALS TOGETHER

———

I would be lying if I said the five of us sit down for a family meal seven nights a week.

DAVE: *You'd be lying if you said the five of us sit down for a family meal* two *nights a week.*

It's true. One of us will typically feed the kids early, and Dave and I will have a bite after they're in bed. But every once in a while, we pick a night where our family time revolves around food. It's not always the same, but it's always fun, and no matter how old or what crazy stage our kids are at, they quickly settle in to hanging out around our kitchen island.

So how do we accommodate a pescatarian, a vegetarian, two meat eaters, and a vegan?

DAVE: *Does it involve a priest and a rabbi walking into a bar?*

KORTNEY: *No, but if anyone wants to send prayers, I welcome them.*

Four DIY Family Meals

1. **Top your own taco.** Nothing revolutionary here, except that we do this 100 percent buffet style, laying out hard tacos, soft tacos, meat for the man-boys, and 10 kinds of toppings. Grab a plate and it's every hombre for himself.

2. **Make your own Mediterranean.** This is Sully's favorite. He loves that there's really no cooking involved, just a massive platter of olives, crackers, hummus, cheese, grapes, fresh veggies, and salami. During the warm months, we enjoy Mediterranean nights outside on the lawn, and in the winter, we spread a blanket on the floor and have a pretend picnic by the sea.

3. **Personal pizzas.** Jett lives for pizza night. We buy the dough from our local pizza parlor and roll it out ourselves. The topping buffet bar comes in handy once again, allowing us to make individual pizzas for every person. Prefer a thin crust? No problem. Roll it out a little more, buddy. Craving extra meat? Pile on the pepperoni. Or smile and say "vegan cheese."

4. **Not yo nachos, my nachos.** Lennox and I both claim this night as our personal favorite, and it's all about the toppings. We take little pie tins and each person starts with some chips. I top them with everything from crispy tofu to olives and onions, then layer on the cheese. I toss it in the oven to melt and crisp up, and it's THE BEST THING EVER. The kids go for the chicken, or beans and rice, and Dave is a glutton for hot sauce punishment. It really doesn't matter. The point is, we're all in the kitchen reaching and prepping and double-dipping *together*.

SPARK CONVERSATION

When all three kids were little, we couldn't get them to *stop* talking. But as they've grown older, not all conversations flow quite as freely. A teenager can talk about tennis shoes until his tongue falls off, but if you try to engage him on the subject of school or study habits or other *fascinating* topics that begin with the letter "S," suddenly he's capable of speaking only in grunts and single syllables.

While it won't work every time, I've found that rephrasing questions to avoid yes or no answers helps tremendously, particularly with kids in that 7-to-10 age range who haven't yet mastered the exasperated eye roll.

DAVE: *What are you talking about? Lennox mastered the exasperated eye roll back in kindergarten.*

KORTNEY: *She's gifted.*

For what it's worth, I've trained myself to rephrase these popular parental inquiries as follows:

- Instead of "How was school?" try "What was your favorite part of the day?"

- Instead of "Are you excited for tomorrow?" try "What's one thing you're looking forward to tomorrow?"

- Instead of "Were you good today?" or "Did you behave?" try "How did you help someone today?"

- Instead of "Who did you play with?" try "Who at school could be nicer to you?"

When kids want to talk but don't know how to broach a subject, open-ended or guiding questions like these can help grease the skids.

Another thing we do from time to time, when the kids will tolerate it, is take turns pulling questions from the conversation jar. This almost always solicits sighs and groans at first, but as soon as we get them talking, they get caught up in the conversation and forget how *lame* and *boring* Dave and I can be.

You can buy conversation cards online or at toy stores—or make them yourself. Mine were an impulse purchase, but we've since added questions of our own to keep it interesting. Everyone in the family contributed 10 questions, and we pull one out at the start of a

sit-down dinner to get the conversation (and yes, sometimes the eyes) rolling.

Where should we go on our next family vacation?

What's your biggest fear?

If you could relive one moment in history, what moment would you choose?

DAVE: *And without fail, they'll choose a moment that involved you buying them candy or shoes.*

KORTNEY: *I said it was a conversation jar. Not a "deep conversation" jar.*

If you're looking to make a soul connection with every conversation, you're probably going to be disappointed. Kids are going to be kids no matter what method you use to draw them out. But I'm a firm believer that when it comes to talking to your kids, quantity *is* quality. And when they feel like they can talk to you about the silly stuff, the big stuff becomes less of a leap.

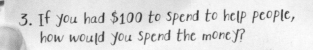

3. If you had $100 to spend to help people, how would you spend the money?

KIDIBBLE FOR DISH DUTY

—

I'm a mildly competitive person.

DAVE: *Ha-ha-ha-ha-ha, oh. That's a good one. Mildly competitive.*

KORTNEY: *What?*

DAVE: *Oh, you were serious? About the "mildly"? I thought you were—never mind. "Mildly" competitive it is.*

I like games. And I love to laugh. So any activity that combines the two is *right* up my alley.

DAVE: *And, to be clear, she is going to mop that alley with all of our faces.*

KORTNEY: *I am a worthy adversary.*

DAVE: *You are a tiny and devious parlor-game dictator who hates to lose.*

KORTNEY: *Tomato, tomahto.*

If there's one thing Dave and I *do* agree on, it's that neither of us wants to do the dishes.

Especially after a huge family meal with multiple courses. That's where Kidibble comes in. Why we started calling it Kidibble is anyone's guess, but it started after Thanksgiving dinner one year when all 12 of us—parents, brothers, sisters, kids—were jockeying to escape the dreaded dish duty. Someone came up with the genius idea to "kidibble" for it, and a family tradition was born.

How to Play Kidibble

1. The more people you have, the more fun it is. Everyone at the table gets three raw pasta noodles. Three of any small object will work: nickels, dried beans, whatever can be concealed in the palm of your hand.

2. Everyone at the table secretly puts zero to three noodles in their right hand and puts their closed fist on the table. (So, if there are 10 people at the table, there is potential to have up to 30 noodles in hands.)

3. Starting with the oldest (or youngest, or—ahem—most competitive), you go around the table and everyone guesses how many noodles there are in hands in total. Once a

number is guessed, no one else can guess it. There are no ties in Kidibble.

4. You'll start to notice that if a bunch of people in a row guess low numbers, they likely have a low number of noodles in their hand and the total will be, well, *lower*.

5. After you've gone around the table once, everyone opens their hand to reveal what they have. Whoever guessed the closest wins the round and is excused from dish duty and from the table (though most winners stick around to see who the big loser will be).

6. Repeat until there's no one left but the unlucky dishwasher.

My favorite memory of this game is when it came down to my dad and me. There were potentially six noodles between us, and it was his turn to guess first. He guessed zero, and I knew I had lost right then, because I had *none* in my hand, and obviously he did too. The crowd went wild.

DAVE: *Did you cry?*

KORTNEY: *I did not cry! I love to win, but I'm definitely not a sore loser.*

Fair is fair, and it's all in good fun. (And if my mom—aka the grand champion Kidibbler—is in the room like she was that day, she will always take pity on the loser and help load.)

NEVER BUY
A FOREVER SOFA

Because a sofa is a big piece of furniture—and a big expense—many of us set out to find a "forever sofa," something that will work for us and our families no matter how our spaces and lives change. Not only is that approach overly daunting, it's just not practical. Your life *will* change. Guaranteed. And your space will evolve with it. You are far more likely to find a sofa that makes you happy longer if you buy it with "today" in mind. Trying to hedge your bets by purchasing something that will "work no matter what happens in the future" is likely to backfire, leaving you with a sofa you feel only so-so about. Do yourself a favor and find the perfect "now sofa." Focus on what you love *today* and take the future (and the pressure) out of the equation.

BE CLEVER
WITH CURTAINS

People always ask me where I got the curtains for our kitchen, and I love to see the happy surprise on their faces when I reveal my sources. We live in an old Victorian home with 14-foot ceilings, so finding off-the-shelf panels that accommodate that height is not really an option. Custom curtains, on the other hand, are extremely pricey, and for me—and so many people—they just aren't in the budget. Which is how I came up with this clever curtain hack: Buy two standard panels off the shelf, one spotted and one solid, and sew them together lengthwise. A very simple drapery rod and similarly simple drapery clip rings (a totally acceptable solution) and *bam!* Fourteen-foot curtains that look custom, for little more than $60, all in.

DAVE: *Do you have a picture of yourself slaving over the sewing machine to inspire our readers?*

KORTNEY: *No, but I have a picture of my* mother *slaving over the sewing machine for me, because she loves me and is a much better seamstress than I am.*

DAVE: *I slipped her $50 under the table for that.*

KORTNEY: *You did not.*

Here's the thing. While I got extra lucky having a mom who loves to sew, hiring a seamstress to sew two ready-made panels in a straight line is a lot more affordable than buying fabric and having curtains made from scratch.

DAVE: *You're holding out on us. I can feel it.*

KORTNEY: *What are you talking about?*

DAVE: *You have a secret. You're wearing your "I have a secret" face.*

KORTNEY: *I don't have an "I have a secret" face.*

DAVE: *You do! It's so obvious. You have a curtain secret, and you are a tiny bit evil, and you don't want to share it.*

KORTNEY: *David Wilson.*

DAVE: *Spill it.*

KORTNEY: *You are ridiculous.*

DAVE: *Draw back the curtain on your curtain secret . . .*

It's not even a secret! And it's not my first choice. But it is a super handy option to complete your room on a budget: iron-on hemming tape (which is essentially two-sided fabric tape that activates when you iron it) will be your saving grace, especially if you can't sew to save your life.

Top 10 "Secrets" for Curtain-Hanging Success

1. **Keep the hemming tape handy.** Yes, you can use hemming tape to "sew" two panels together. But it's especially handy if you're just shortening your curtains and want to achieve a nice clean line without a lot of hassle.

    KORTNEY: *And yes, Dave, people will notice if you just cut the curtains and leave the raw edge at the bottom.*

    DAVE: *I didn't even say anything!*

    KORTNEY: *You didn't have to. You were wearing your "just cut the curtains and leave the raw edge at the bottom" face.*

    DAVE: *I totally was.*

2. **The higher the better. (Most of the time.)** There are exceptions to the rule (like when the trim, crown molding, or curtain rod is so spectacular you want to show it off), but *most of the time*, I like to hang curtains as close to the ceiling as possible for a more dramatic look. This is especially important if your ceilings are lower, because curtains draw the eye upward, making the whole room look bigger.

3. **Don't let your husband hang the curtain rods unless you're in the room.** He will try to impress you by lining up the ends of the rod with the sides of the windows. Spoiler alert: you will not be impressed. The curtain rod should extend *at least* 3 inches (7.5 centimeters) beyond the window, though often I take them out even further, spanning nearly the entire length of the wall.

4. **Curtains should simply kiss the floor,** not lounge like a man watching Monday night football, or stand like soldiers at attention. They should just *barely* touch, so you get maximum height and just a hint of movement. It's a tiny detail that makes all the difference.

No

Yes

5. **Make them machine washable.** I'm a wash-and-go girl whenever and wherever possible, and that goes for curtains too. Kids, pets, and everyday dust can take a toll on even the toughest fabrics, and the last thing I want to do is haul curtains to the dry cleaner when they start to get dingy. That said, if you've taken to heart my tip about the hemming tape, you might be wise to avoid the washing machine altogether and stick with spot-cleaning. Hemming tape is magic, but it's not a miracle, and it might not withstand more than one round in the wash.

6. **Curtains don't have to be curtains.** Consider hanging curtains as dividers in your kids' bedroom. If they share a room and the space is large enough, you can give them each some privacy. Even a set of clean white sheers can section off a room while still maintaining a feeling of openness and space. There are a variety of ways to treat curtains as dividers, but I recommend using the hardware made especially for this purpose, which installs into the ceiling.

7. **When in doubt, do white curtains with black rods.** Hanging curtains that are the wrong color is way worse than having no curtains at all. If you're having trouble trusting your instincts—or you have a room that gets a lot of change in light—you really can't go wrong with white curtains on a black rod. It's simple, it's classic, and it goes with pretty much anything.

8. **Panels should be twice the width of the window** (assuming you're going to leave them open). If your window is 30 inches (75 centimeters), you should have at least 60 inches (1.5 meters) of panels. This is one area where less is definitely not more, so always err on the side of fullness. When I see skimpy panels dangling on either side of a wide window, it reminds me of bad haircuts that poorly frame the face.

9. **Choose patterns wisely.** I'm all about mixing patterns, but if your furniture is patterned, you should consider solid panels that complement the main colors in the dominant pattern. On the other hand, if your furniture and linens are all solid, you may consider enlivening the space with a large-scale pattern.

10. **Keep them open!** Curtains are meant to frame the window, not swallow it whole. If you need your curtains to be more functional, you'll want each panel to be at least *three* times the width of the entire window, so when they are closed, they don't look like you hung a bedsheet flat across the window. If at all possible, get some blinds and let the curtains do their job of creating symmetry, balance, and beauty to pull the room together.

MOVE OVER, MAN CAVES

———

The phrase "man cave" has been around for as long as I can remember, but I never gave it much thought before I got married and had children. Now that I'm a mom, I can't help but roll my eyes when I hear of men retreating to their special man place to watch a game, drink a beer, or listen to music lady-free. Not because I don't think the men in the family deserve a place to get away, but because women need it so much more.

DAVE: *Bam. She said it.*

KORTNEY: *Sue me, but it's true.*

Not a day goes by where I couldn't use a little alone time. And I'm not even looking for a place to relax—I need a man cave so I can *work* in peace. As all mothers know, kids have no sense of boundaries. I can't even take a shower without one of our kids walking in to ask me a question. They don't even notice that I'm standing there naked with soap in my eyes. They keep right on talking. And I keep right on answering, because *I have soap in my eyes and I want them to go away!*

I love being a mom, and I love being needed, but when "she sheds" entered the design vernacular, I was on board with both feet. While man caves are hulking affairs with thick leather sofas and complex sound systems and big-screen TVs, the she shed is just my speed. Primitive and pretty and, *most important*, too small for tiny visitors.

It can be a place to work or take a private phone call, or a place to retreat with a glass of wine while you catch up on *Grey's Anatomy*. All the better if it's not under the main roof, so no one else can claim it as their own.

When I see a shed that would otherwise be torn down, I see an opportunity to give some lucky lady a place where she doesn't have to roll her eyes (unless she wants to).

My first she-shed renovation was so well received that I try to recreate it every time there's an opportunity. For as little as $500, I've converted garden sheds that were about to be torn down into "rooms of one's own" that Virginia Woolf would have written home about.

She-Shed Pointers

- **Let there be light.** Every she shed should have natural light. Granted, you may be trying to hide, but at least give yourself the option to see the sun. God made dead bolts and Do Not Disturb signs for a reason.

- **Resurface the interior walls.** If the walls look shedlike, a little shiplap or beadboard will do just the trick.

- **Have somewhere soft to sit or lie down.** A little napping loft, or even a cozy chair *just for one*, will be perfect. Remember: you're not trying to entice others to join you.

- **Add a pretty little rug and a reading lamp,** and that's really all you need. There's no reason to go overboard with the design unless you *really* want to.

I like my she sheds to be casual, convenient, and not in the least bit fussy. The whole point of the she shed is to get away from it all. So don't overthink it or overdesign it. If your she shed plays multiple roles—say, part art studio, part voluntary confinement—that's perfectly okay, because no one else has to use or love this space but you. For me personally, "minimalism" would be the magic word, so you can arrive at your happy place as quickly as womanly possible.

REAP WHILE YOU SOW

We have an edible garden. Basil, cilantro, parsley, tomatoes, rhubarb. Well, we used to have rhubarb.

DAVE: *I should have listened to you about the rhubarb. It just looked like it needed a trim.*

KORTNEY: *You trimmed it alright. Trimmed it dead.*

DAVE: *I've learned my rhubarb lesson.*

Dave doesn't like the garden. He thinks it's too much work for too little reward. And he makes a fair point. Gardens are delicate, Tennessee summers are hot, and we do travel quite a bit.

DAVE: *And the grocery store is RIGHT THERE. We can see it from our house.*

KORTNEY: *It's not the same.*

DAVE: *You're right. We don't have to water the basil at the grocery store.*

This is true. When you pour precious weekend hours into tending your little crop, you have to hire someone over the age of seven to remember to water it while you're away. And no one can leave the chickens out in the yard all day, or they'll see your gardening efforts as an all-you-can-eat buffet. We've learned these lessons the hard way, and yet . . . I still have my beloved garden.

Even in the winter months, when nothing's growing, I'm glad it's there. We have a small backyard that we use every inch of, so I wanted the garden to be pretty all year round. We built these raised garden beds—waist-high for easy tending and poor chicken access. After the cedarwood aroma wore off, I stained the beds in three different shades so they'd be gorgeous to look at even in the off-season.

Here's the thing. The work of planting and nurturing the garden is part of the joy for me. I love seeing the little seedlings bud and having to add the stakes as they get taller. I love pinching the flower buds off my basil. I love tending my tomatoes and watching them ripen in the sun. I love stepping out the back door and having all the makings of a perfect pesto. I love sharing a basket of fresh-picked tomatoes with my neighbors. I love it all. And so the work isn't just worth it—the work *is* it. They say you reap what you sow. I also reap *while* I sow.

PICK A FLOOR, ANY FLOOR (BUT ONLY ONE)

Most interior designers will tell you not to have more than three transitions in your home's flooring. I take that recommendation a step further and say the fewer the better, with the best-case scenario being *none*. Think about it. The floor *literally* grounds the entire home design, so the fewer transitions from room to room, the more fun you can have with the decor itself. If at all possible, I will use the same flooring throughout the entire house, with the only exception being bathrooms.

With bathroom floors, feel free to mix it up. As long as they're in keeping with the rest of the house stylistically, each bathroom can have a different tile without sacrificing your home's flow. In fact, I *prefer* to change up the flooring from bathroom to bathroom, because it adds character and prevents the bathrooms from appearing like an afterthought.

DAVE: *So why are bathrooms the exception?*

KORTNEY: *Because of their function.*

DAVE: *Ah. You mean, their "duty"?*

KORTNEY: *Dave, can you pretend to be a big boy right now, please?*

DAVE: *You didn't answer the question.*

KORTNEY: *The reason is this: Two bathrooms will rarely sit beside each other, so their flooring won't be competing. Also, different bathrooms serve different members of the household. For example, the kids' bathroom may have slip-resistant tile, while the master suite will have something more luxurious.*

While you want the rest of the house to flow seamlessly from one room to the next, you actually want a bathroom to feel separate, because it gives a feeling of privacy. The transition in this case serves a legitimate purpose. There's also the obvious practical reason, which is that bathroom floors are more at risk of water damage and do best with tile floors. I can't tell you how many plumbers have given me the hairy eyeball just for having hardwoods in the half-baths, but that's a risk I'm willing to take.

Hardwood floors are my number one choice in almost every home design scenario. Hallways, living rooms, dining rooms, bedrooms, common areas, and kitchens (YES, kitchens) look beautiful with hardwoods. Their rich natural color is very grounding, and they complement every style of furniture and decor. They last longer than carpet, they're easier to keep clean, and they can be refinished if they become overly worn. While I do love bamboo and other prefinished flooring options, a simple finished oak floor is never going to go out of style.

I've been in 26,000-square-foot mansions that have incredible custom flooring with specialty patterns and inlays that transition from room to room, and I still don't love it. It's overpowering and draws your eyes and all of the energy in the room *downward*. When floors have that much dominance in a room, it feels unnatural and a bit unsettling.

If you love carpet and can't live without it, I say: the same rule applies. Pick *one* wall-to-wall carpet you absolutely love and use it throughout the house. You can shake it up a bit by layering area rugs on top to define each room.

The Scoop on Flooring Layout

When we're working on old houses, we are often dealing with old hardwood flooring and even older subflooring (or no subflooring at all). In these cases, we'll run the flooring perpendicular to the floor joists, so the boards are better supported. As long as the subfloor is strong, however, you don't *have* to run the boards perpendicular to the joists. In general, I like to run flooring from the front of the house to the back, so the lines draw you in and through the house. This is not a hard-and-fast rule, though. Sometimes you just need to live with it a bit before you make a decision. And since flooring needs to acclimate to the house before you lay it, I always use that time to look at the flooring both ways before I commit.

Personally, I prefer to run all of the flooring in the same direction throughout the rooms. Remember, the fewer transitions, the better the flow. But if you have a particularly high-traffic area, like a kitchen, keep in mind that you will need to refinish it before the rest of the house, so you might deliberately lay the boards in the opposite direction so you can just refinish that room when the time comes. It's not my first choice, but it's not the end of the world. Again, the "rules" are here to serve you, not stress you out.

GET REAL ABOUT RUGS

———

I know rugs are important. I use them every day in staging to bring warmth to rooms and make them feel complete. I love rugs, but I hardly have any in my house. And the ones I do have are inexpensive and small enough to fit in a front-loader washing machine.

Rugs are beautiful. Rugs are *comfortable*. And if you have kids, pets, friends who drink wine, or any combination thereof, rugs are *impossible* to keep clean.

So I've given up (for now). And I hereby give you permission to do the same. If your lifestyle is not conducive to rugs, don't have rugs. The same goes for any of the tips in this book. Good design is meant to *enhance* your life, not burden it. And you are the master of your domain, not the other way around. For me, at this point in my life, the luxurious area rugs I love are a burden not worth bearing.

But! For those of you rug lovers who are more in the "can't live with them, can't live without them" camp, read on.

Rug Pointers

MULTICOLOR RUGS

When was the last time you stayed in a hotel where the carpet was one solid color? My guess is never. And there's a good (if not unsettling) reason for that. Hotel rugs are *riddled with stains*.

You just can't see the stains, because the kooky patterns and colors keep your eyes from focusing on them. The same concept applies here, but to a slightly lesser degree. Rugs with lots of colors hide stains and stay lively longer. They also give you *tons* of options for the rest of the room, which is an added bonus. Typically the rug is the last thing purchased, which can make it hard to get a multicolor rug exactly right. But if you're on the front side of a renovation and you find a rug that you love, consider designing from the ground up, building the rest of the color palette from that foundation.

OVERLAPPING LAYERS

This is a trick I use all the time with staging in order to get maximum impact for the minimum cost. I'll find a large area rug that's less expensive and neutral in color, then layer a smaller, more colorful, and intricate design on top. The larger rug creates a border around it and enables me to follow all of the rug rules pertaining to size (hold your horses; I'll give you these in a second) and coverage, without spending a fortune. For high-traffic homes subject to kids,

pets, and parties, this technique can also be a winner. Center a smaller, washable accent rug on your larger neutral one—or layer multiple small (and did I say washable?) rugs to create a layered area you can keep clean. Or, at least, keep cleaning.

SEAGRASS RUGS

While they're not machine washable, seagrass rugs can be spot-cleaned fairly easily thanks to their less absorbent fibers. Their textured weave and natural color variations hide stains for a much lower cost than wool.

CARPET TILES

For me, these took a little getting used to, and I don't *always* love the look. But if you choose the right color combination, these "plug and play" tiles are a super practical way to soften up a high-traffic area. If one square becomes overly worn or unsightly, just replace it and keep the rest of the rug intact.

HANDWOVEN COTTON THROW RUGS

I love these little devils. They're inexpensive, colorful, and (most important) machine washable. They're the only rugs you'll find on my floors at home, unless of course they're awaiting their turn in the laundry room, which is more than likely. You will need to invest in a quality rug pad to keep them in place, or you will be in for an unwelcome magic carpet ride.

Quick Tips for Sizing and Placement

Size matters. Ideally the rug will be big enough so that all of the furniture legs in the room stand on the rug. If you can't quite swing that (big rugs are expensive, I know), make sure the front legs are all on board. In the dining room, however, I have to be more of a stickler. All the chair legs need to rest on the rug when people are seated, so there's no unpleasant wibbly-wobbling while you're trying to eat.

Leave a border. In larger rooms, you'll want to leave a border of 18 to 24 inches (45 to 60 centimeters) around your rug. In smaller rooms or walk-in closets, reduce the border width to less than a foot, and it will make the room feel bigger.

Extend beyond the bed. Rugs should extend at least 12 inches (30 centimeters) beyond a twin bed on all sides and 18 inches (45 centimeters) for queens and kings. More is even better. A smaller rug can also work at the foot of the bed, to add an accent and ground the room. Just make sure it extends beyond the width of the bed to balance the space.

Double up. In big rooms, you don't have to order a massive custom area rug. Instead, choose two smaller rugs to fill the floor and create separate areas of activity.

STICK IT TO YOUR WALLS

Believe it or not, I have fond memories of removing wallpaper with my mom and sisters when I was little. This was in the '70s, when wallpaper was *everywhere,* and every time my parents bought a new house, they quickly determined that the wallpaper was an abomination that had to go. So the three of us would set to work, soaking the walls in warm water, peeling the paper, and repeating the process over and over (and over again) until the paper came completely off. As much as I (begrudgingly) enjoyed those many hours of girl time, this tedious and mind-numbing work was not something I welcomed into adulthood. I was more than happy when wallpaper was deemed a definitive design no-no. But today, like my leopard-print pants from the '90s (which I thought were destined for that great costume closet in the sky), wallpaper has made a serious comeback. And unlike leopard print, it's going to be here awhile. I *railed* against this resurgence for years, but then the patterns, *the colors*, and the possibilities became too much to resist.

Although the old-school wallpaper is still alive and well (and there are tools and chemicals to help you remove it a *bit* faster), there are also plenty of peel-and-stick options that will serve you well in many applications—not just *walls*.

Where to Wallpaper

- **The ceiling.** If it's a room where you'd consider painting the ceiling a fun color, then it's a place to consider wallpaper. The rest of the walls need to be fairly neutral—or at least free of distractions. Alternatively, I've seen people paper the wall opposite the room's entrance and continue that paper overhead, so it's one continuous line, and it works beautifully.

- **Staircase risers.** A great way to update older staircases, wallpapered risers are a cute and quirky conversation piece. I prefer to see this treatment in rec rooms or playrooms, or maybe the staircase from a main floor to a livable basement, since the effect tends to be more playful than elegant.

- **The bathroom backsplash.** A good vinyl wallpaper checks the form and function boxes when it comes to the bathroom backsplash wall. Toothpaste and water splashes wipe off in a snap and the wall becomes an interesting focal point for the room. Try painting your vanity a fun color, like cobalt blue, and find a coordinating blue-and-white

wallpaper to carry up to the ceiling behind it. Not a fan of color? No problem. A black vanity and coordinating geometric-patterned paper works just as well.

- **Shelf walls.** I love the look of wallpaper in an open pantry or built-in shelves. Paper the entire wall or choose one or two shelves to accent. Alternatively, you can mix and match coordinating colors and patterns from one shelf to the next. Because these walls are a backdrop to the items placed *on* the shelves, you can get away with bold prints and lively patterns without them overwhelming the space.

- **In a frame.** I've always been a sucker for scale, but large art can get pretty pricey. I was looking for an oversize piece of art to set off a wall with a vaulted ceiling in a house we were flipping recently, but the ones I loved were way out of our budget. So, we found peel-and-stick wallpaper with a fun, loose geometric print and used it to cover a piece of smooth plywood, cut to size. Framed and hung, it gave the room just the touch of drama I wanted—without the hefty price tag. (See DIY on the next page.)

Now that I've encouraged you to be creative with the myriad wallpaper options available, let me say this: there are some things that should *never*, under any circumstances, be covered in wallpaper. Having flipped over 100 houses in 12 years, Dave and I have seen pretty much everything. And these five wallpaper transgressions are ones I wish I could unsee. Truly. They *haunt* me like a ghost. A ghost covered in wallpaper.

Where NOT to Wallpaper

- **The trim.** It's called trim for a reason, friends. Trim means "border." And borders are meant to *frame* the room. So if you paper a wall and find yourself feeling like the trim should match . . . you need to *unfeel that feeling* immediately.

- **The outlet covers.** If your outlet covers are so ugly you feel the need to cover them in wallpaper, sell your leftover paper and buy yourself some new outlet covers. This is a capital-"N" No-No.

- **The entire bathroom.** And by "entire bathroom," I mean the walls, the tile, and the shower curtain rod. You laugh, but Dave and I have seen it. More than once.

- **The floor.** Just, no.

- **The refrigerator.** I don't care how ugly your fridge is; I promise you, wallpaper will only make it worse. Why? Because a refrigerator is shaped like a box. And a box covered in wallpaper looks an awful lot like a giant present waiting to be unwrapped. Emphasis on the word "awful."

DIY WALLPAPER ART

If you want the impact of large-scale art without the blow to your budget, wallpaper can be a price-conscious alternative. For this tutorial, I'm going to keep it super simple and recommend you use peel-and-stick wallpaper in the color and pattern of your choice. You can find a plethora of options at most big-box stores and any online home decor retailer.

1. **Pick a print.** Any print. If it makes you smile and fits within your color scheme, go for it. Art is subjective, so if the pattern pleases you, let your gut be your guide and try not to overthink it.

2. **Cut plywood to size.** Your local hardware store can cut a piece of smooth plywood to the size of your choice. The thinner and lighter it is, the easier it will be to hang.

3. **Center the wallpaper.** To ensure a repeating pattern is centered, draw a vertical line down the center of your board, so the board is divided into two equal halves. Align the edge of your first strip of paper to your center line and align the remaining strips to that one. This way, your pattern will not be lopsided.

4. **Smooth your wallpaper over the plywood, making sure to wrap it around the edges of the board.** (I like to have at least about 2 inches, or 5 centimeters, wrapping around the back of the board, so I can secure the paper with pins or staples.)

5. **Use a credit card or ruler to smooth out the bubbles.** You can buy a fancy tool for this, but, like I said, we're keeping it simple.

6. **Secure the paper from the back.** Keep in mind that peel-and-stick wallpaper is designed to be removed easily, which means it's not stuck hard and fast. I use glazier point pushpins, a staple gun, or thumbtacks to secure the paper to the board in back. Three per side should do the trick.

7. **Frame it.** If it's in the budget, a frame will do wonders to complete the piece. But if the objective is to get a cool piece of art on a big old empty wall as quickly and inexpensively as possible, keep it simple and skip this step.

8. **Hang that baby up!** A standard picture-hanging kit will give you everything you need for just a few dollars. Two screw eyes, some braided wire, and a hook and nail and you're good to go.

TREAT THE CEILING
LIKE A FIFTH WALL

Not only is it acceptable to paint a ceiling in dark or vibrant colors, I encourage it. There's no design law that states all ceilings must be white, and yet, in new construction and old, white ceilings seem to be the standard. Taking a sharp left turn and kicking up the color a notch is a great way to get a "high design" look without breaking the bank.

I just painted the entire upstairs ceiling of a loft black, and the result is stunning. It's unexpected, for sure, but the monochromatic palette of the home's interior was minimalistic enough that a black ceiling made perfect sense. It's all about balance. In the case of this particular loft, the kitchen cabinets were solid black with white interiors and glass panes. ALL of the walls in the main areas were painted a cool white. In order to balance the space, I knew I needed to weave the black back in, and in a big way. The vaulted ceiling called to me. As crazy as it might sound, it was that black ceiling that grounded the design and kept the white walls from disappearing.

If you're ready to go bold overhead, neutrals are not your only option. In one of our recent flips—where the interior decor was primary-color dominant—I painted the ceiling a fiery red to reinforce the room's symmetry. I knew there was a chance it wouldn't work (too much red runs the risk of giving your space, and everyone in it, a case of the angries), but as I always say, *it's only paint*, so go big or . . . go back to the store and try another color!

Paint is not the only way to address your fifth wall. Peel-and-stick paneling, barnboard, coffered ceilings, tin, shiplap, wallpaper, and even tile are all viable ways to add visual interest and character to your ceiling. And if color and texture *don't* feel quite right, a beautiful medallion mounted around a light fixture on a white or off-white ceiling is an elegant addition that never goes out of style.

The main takeaway here is that every inch of your house belongs to you—so *own it* and get creative with that precious overhead real estate.

MAKE MAGIC
WITH MIRRORS

———

Mirrors are a designer's best friend. They can create depth in small rooms, brighten rooms with limited natural light, and provide a focal point in rooms that have none. If placed properly in a room, they can accomplish all three objectives. Just remember to strive for "fun" instead of "fun house" and limit mirrors to surfaces that make sense.

Cautions for Mirrors

- **Mirrors need to be cleaned.** Regularly. If you're the type who's lax about cleaning the mirror over your bathroom sink, you're not going to love cleaning a collection of mirrors over your living room sofa.

- **Kids + mirrors = fingerprints *squared*.** Unless you're a glutton for punishment, you'll keep mirrors to a minimum wherever kids can be found.

- **Mirrors and pets don't always mix.** Some dogs will bark incessantly at their reflections. This is great for hilarious Instagram videos and *really annoying* for homeowners who have mirrored walls. So beware.

Two Mirror Must-Haves

In your bedroom. A full-length, freestanding mirror as wide as the bedroom can handle is optimal. It's the one place private enough to give yourself a thorough once-over, so splurge on a good-size mirror (preferably framed) that both looks beautiful and captures *all* of your beauty in its reflection. If space is limited, a mirror hung on the inside of the closet door will do the trick just fine.

And don't forget about your guest room! Visitors want to make sure they look presentable too. Don't make them sneak into your bedroom to do it.

In your entranceway. Remember that drop spot we talked about? The one where you keep your keys and sunglasses so they never get lost? The drop spot is also a great place to stop and give

yourself a once-over before you go out in public. Add a mirror there, so you can extract any stray nose hairs or wipe lipstick from your teeth.

Unexpected Mirror Options

Kitchen islands. If you're lucky enough to live in an ultra-modern (kid-free, pet-free) house, you might consider an island with mirrored sides. You'd still have your choice of countertop; the base on which it sits is framed entirely with mirrored glass. The effect, when done well, is that the island almost disappears as it reflects the room around it and gives the illusion of open space.

Walls. In the '80s and '90s, mirrored walls and closets were all the rage, and as a house flipper, I've seen (and demolished!) my fair share. In general, mirrored walls are extremely difficult to do well, but small spaces can benefit from the optical illusion mirrors create. In a small, ultra-modern space, a mirrored accent wall can trick the eye and double the look of your space. In more traditional homes, wide-framed closet doors with mirrors are a nice update to the fully mirrored sliding doors of yore.

Gallery walls. Exposed brick might seem like an imposing surface, but it's one of my favorite backdrops for a mirror gallery wall. The texture contrast of brick and glass is just gorgeous. If you don't have exposed brick, you can accomplish a similar effect with wallpaper, shiplap, or peel-and-stick wood. If you choose high-quality surface coverings, the realism will surprise you. A mirror gallery wall works in just about any room (except the kitchen); just be sure to avoid light-colored frames on light-colored walls. Since the mirror is only reflecting the rest of the room (unlike, say, a work of art), it needs that contrasting border to keep it from disappearing. Try a collection of antique mirrors you find at the flea market. Or buy a bunch of mirrors and paint the frames gold. They don't all have to be the same shape or color—the mirrors themselves will create continuity.

Bathroom windows. A mirror in front of a bathroom window? Has she lost her mind? Not this time. I know it defies my usual logic, but if you hang a mirror from the ceiling, in front of a window, so the light shines all around it, you will have the *perfect* makeup mirror, with even natural light. Just be sure to select a mirror size smaller than the window, so it looks deliberate and isn't blocking out the light.

Tile backsplashes. It comes back to texture. Smooth mirror glass, textured tile—always a win. I'm especially fond of round frameless mirrors hung above rectangular vanities. They take the edge off a room with lots of square angles and bring balance and calm.

Mirror No-Nos

Facing the toilet. You'd think this would be a no-brainer, but I see it all the time. Who wants to look at themselves in the mirror while they're . . . you know what? Don't answer that. Let's move on.

Behind the bed. Just because a mirror happens to be the same *width* as a headboard, doesn't mean it was born to *be* a headboard. I'm no expert in feng shui, but a mirror behind my head while I sleep feels ominous somehow. I judge myself enough during the day. The last thing I need is my own reflection lurking over my shoulder while I sleep.

At the end of a hallway. This seems like a good idea in theory—empty wall, practical and convenient placement. But I've tried it in enough houses to know that it just doesn't work. A hallway is a transitional space, so it focuses your mind on where you're *going*. When you catch your own reflection unexpectedly, it startles you. Every time.

The ceiling. Bow chicka, bow chicka—NO. Dave and I once stayed in a hotel room that had a massive mirror on the ceiling over the bed. It was so disconcerting, I wanted to sleep with a pillowcase over my head.

DAVE: *I take offense to that. I kind of liked it.*

KORTNEY: *Well, by the second night, we made it work.*

DAVE: *They don't call us the masters of flip for nothin'.*

KORTNEY: *Okay. ENOUGH.*

I'm all about making magic with mirrors, but this look has Larry Flynt written all over it. I just think mirrors on ceilings don't have any place in home decor.

In the kitchen. With the exception of the ultra-modern mirrored island (which, let's face it, is also pretty impractical, but still *awesome*), mirrors just don't make sense in the kitchen. They make a busy space even busier, reflecting the energy and activity around them. And, did I mention they need to be cleaned? I've seen people place mirrors over the stove and it gives me hives just thinking about it. If you're longing for a reflective surface in this particular spot, try some stainless steel tile. I promise it will be just as difficult to clean, and if you look hard enough, you will see yourself.

BATHE IN PEACE

Bath time is a sacred tradition in our house. It's one of those rare times you're forced to literally unplug and take full advantage.

How to Make Your Bathroom an Oasis of Calm

Candles, candles, and more candles. I don't understand "one candle" people. One candle is great on a baby's first birthday cake, but it's just not enough light to bathe by. Unless it's just a quick soak, I want to be surrounded. I'll dim the bulbs and light the candles about 15 minutes before I run the water. This way I'll have enough flickering, scented light to see my sanity coming back to me. For bonus vibes, install a beautiful, well-placed mirror to reflect the candlelight (and double the amount of candles you see).

A luxurious bath mat. This doesn't have to be crazy expensive to feel crazy amazing on your feet. Mine was $30, and every time I step on it, I feel like I'm at the spa. Getting in and out of the tub is part of the experience, and the experience is all about the details. This isn't something you have to replace often, so spend an extra $10 or $15 to get the one you really want.

Fill her up. The whole point of a bath is to submerge my stress, not have half of it hovering naked above the waterline. So I fill the tub all the way to the top. That said, there is nothing more annoying than filling the tub as high as it will go, only to sit and listen to the water spill over into the overflow drain and belch like a barfly for the duration of my bath. Not. Acceptable. There's an easy fix for this, folks. It's called an overflow drain cover, and it's worth more than its weight in gold.

Bombs, bubbles, and salts. I go back and forth between them. And sometimes—brace yourselves—I use all three at once. Because I am a crazy, reckless bath-time rebel. It's your bath, baby. Make of it what you will. When I go to the spa (a rare occasion), I get a kick out of trying all the samples and scents, so why not bring that tiny pleasure home? I keep a basket of bombs and salts and bubble baths by the tub to bring a little luxury into the mix.

The bath caddy is everything. Especially if you have a freestanding tub, like we do. We bathing rebels don't like to reach. The caddy keeps everything, including my beverage of choice, right in front of me.

ENJOY A LOO
WITH A VIEW

———

I can't pinpoint exactly when it happened, but at some point in the last decade, home buyers began to demand private enclosures for the toilets in their master bathrooms. I'm pretty sure I'm in the minority on this one, but I find it an insane waste of space to build a bathroom . . . *inside a bathroom*. It makes no sense. Builders will argue with me until they're blue in the face, saying, "People want their privacy when they're going to the bathroom." Yes! I know. That's why God created *bathrooms*.

And if I'm going to design a gorgeous bathroom (which, of course I *am*), I want to enjoy it, whether I'm brushing my teeth or putting on makeup or . . .

DAVE: *Ruling from your throne?*

KORTNEY: *Yes. Exactly.*

Now, we jokingly call it a throne, but that is *not* to say the toilet needs to be the focal point of your gorgeous bathroom. It just doesn't require its *own* room. If I want to be cooped up in a tiny bathroom stall, I'll hit the local gas station. But in my own home? Give me a loo with a view.

GET REAL JOY FROM FAKE PLANTS

Nothing breathes life into a room like live houseplants. They add color, improve the air quality in your home, absorb sound to help with noise reduction, and there's a large body of research that says houseplants can even improve your health and focus. I will always encourage people to incorporate live plants into their interior design when and wherever possible. At the same time, I understand that plants can pose challenges for some people. Perhaps you travel a lot. Or your cats can't resist wreaking havoc with your potting soil. Maybe, despite your best efforts, you're just not a green thumb. While plant lovers may refuse to accept that good people can be bad at plants, it's an unfortunate fact of life for some of us. I've been known to hasten the demise of more than a few potted plants in my day—and it wasn't for lack of trying.

DAVE: *The local nurseries call you Doctor Death.*

KORTNEY: *I'm not that bad.*

DAVE: *Carlos the cactus would beg to differ.*

KORTNEY: *Oh my god. Poor Carlos. He was such a good cactus.*

DAVE: *The best.*

Sometimes you just have to own your weaknesses, critics be damned. And for that reason, I am and always will be an unapologetic fan of fauxtanicals. Stubborn detractors will insist that they can *always* tell the difference, but I'm here to tell you: artificial plants and flowers have come a *long* way, baby. There are so many options, at a variety of price points, and some of them are downright stunning. Not only that, but they can save us black thumbs time, money, and a whole lot of grief.

When You Go Faux

- **Pots are key.** No matter how beautiful and realistic they are, fake plants will always look more real in a pretty pot.

- **Stay away from silk.** If there's one thing silk plants do amazingly well, it's collect dust, so I tend to steer clear of them altogether, opting for plastic or latex instead. Not only are dusty plants a dead giveaway, but who wants to spend time washing plants? Not me. Faux succulents tend to be the best low-budget option because real succulents look almost fake to begin with.

- **A little goes a long way.** Fauxtanicals should be treated as accents only. If your bohemian dream house hungers for a green wall or assemblage of potted plants, real is the only way to go.

- **Placement is important.** As a general rule of thumb, I wouldn't put a fake plant anywhere I wouldn't put a real one. While it's perfectly acceptable to cheat this a bit (for example, certain plants have very specific light needs, and I wouldn't necessarily insist on mirroring those for a fake plant), if you're going faux because you live in a low-light apartment or windowless basement, you might want to reconsider. A cactus blooming in a dark corner isn't fooling anyone.

INDULGE! IT'S NOT EXCESSIVE IF YOU USE IT AND LOVE IT

I grew up with two working parents in a household of six. My parents worked incredibly hard to support us, and we didn't have a lot of luxuries. They stretched their means to provide the things they hadn't had growing up, while teaching us that there were people who worked every bit as hard as they did at jobs that didn't enable them to provide the same for their families. A strong work ethic was ingrained into me early on, not because it guaranteed wealth, but simply because hard work was the right thing to do.

Case in point, when Dave and I met, we were both working multiple jobs while trying to get our individual music careers up and running. We were barely scraping by, and we had no savings and no safety net.

DAVE: *We were a cliché country song. Two kids, living on love and a dream.*

KORTNEY: *And rice and beans.*

DAVE: *Love, a dream, and rice and beans. Why did we never write that song?*

KORTNEY: *It's not too late. We can shut this whole house-flipping thing down...*

DAVE: *I actually kind of like the house-flipping thing, but it's nice to have a hit in your back pocket.*

As the years went on, and our careers shifted, we were finally in a position to enjoy some of the finer things in life. But it made us uncomfortable. If I bought a nice dress for a special event and someone complimented me on it, I felt compelled to supply the details of where I'd found it on clearance. I didn't want people to think I was the kind of person who "wasted" money or took it too lightly. I was almost superstitious about it, not wanting to be perceived as having plenty of money, in case my good fortune should suddenly go away.

Fast-forward to the recent past, when I dreamed up the idea of transforming our bedroom into my dream closet (and subsequently moving our bed into the guest room). Not only do I love clothes and shoes and accessories, but I also love a good bargain—See? I did it again—so I've amassed quite an enviable wardrobe over the years. While sharing a small closet with your husband is hardly the end of the world, it wasn't *ideal*.

DAVE: *You wanted to stab me any time I tried to access the closet at the same time as you.*

KORTNEY: *"Stab" is a strong word.*

DAVE: *Peck my eyeballs out with a stiletto?*

KORTNEY: *Maybe just bop you over the head with my cowboy boots, which you kept pushing out of the way to make room for your hat collection.*

DAVE: *First of all, it's not a "hat collection." I wear a hat every single day. How often do you go square dancing?*

KORTNEY: *I think our readers get the picture.*

I wanted my own closet, and I wanted it done right. At the same time, I felt guilty about wanting something so extravagant. Dave didn't mind the idea, of course. He was keen on it, in fact, because he felt like I *deserved* it.

DAVE: *Or maybe he just wanted more space for his "hat collection."*

Either way, the idea of "deserving" things makes me itch. It implies that there is always fairness where money is concerned. And I know that's not true. Plenty of people deserve a nice closet, but it's just not in the cards to build one. Nevertheless, we had the space, we had the means, and we decided to move forward with my master plan.

When the closet was complete, every piece of clothing I own, every shoe, and every accessory had a place, where I could see it, access it, and dress for the day stress-free. It was exactly what I wanted, and it removed unnecessary stress from our daily routine, almost instantly.

The day we finished it, I was so excited and proud of the design that I posted a photo on social media. It was shared widely, and for the most part, my friends and fans were very complimentary. But those kind words were lost to me in the wake of negativity and criticism that I should have known would come my way. People called me gluttonous and selfish and greedy for having such a room, and it tore me up. I shouldn't have, but I took the post down, because I didn't want to be judged, and because, honestly, some part of me agreed with those people, and I felt guilty and ashamed.

The more I used my closet, though, the more I loved it, and the happier I was we'd built it. It became more than just a closet; it was that elusive "room of my own," where I could have everything just the way I wanted it without anyone else having to accommodate me or step out of the way. I realized that, if I had posted a picture of the same-size room with haphazard racks and clothes piles tossed willy-nilly, no one would have considered that selfish. But because the design was deliberate and beautiful, it *looked* extravagant and it rankled people.

Here's what I believe. I work hard. And I bet you do too. So if you find yourself in a position to treat yourself to something that you will use and love, *go for it*, guilt free and without excuses. Maybe it's a yoga room, or a prayer closet, or a tennis backboard, or a she shed. Maybe it's a gorgeous teacup you find at that little shop with prices that are just out of reach. If you *use it*, it may be a luxury, but it's no longer an extravagance. And if it brings you joy on top, that is what good design is all about.

WARM UP THE FIRELESS FIREPLACE

I have never been a fan of the faux fireplace. A fireplace that's nonoperational is one thing, but flat-out pretending there's a fireplace *behind* the drywall and framing it with a mantel is just odd. When you frame a fireplace where there isn't one, you're deliberately drawing attention to something that doesn't exist and asking people to play along.

DAVE: *Our wall thinks she's a fireplace. EVERYONE, ACT NATURAL.*

KORTNEY: *Exactly.*

If you *must* fake a fireplace, there should at least be an *opening* where a fire and logs could theoretically fit.

Having lived in historic homes for the past 15 years, I've grown accustomed to nonoperational fireplaces, and I wouldn't dream of covering them up. But just because there's no fire happening inside doesn't mean they can't be used to warm up a room.

Before we get into the *how* of fireless fireplaces, let's talk for a minute about placement. Ideally, the fireplace will be the focal point of the room. Furniture should still be placed *as if* the fireplace is operational. That means either a sofa facing the fireplace, or dueling sofas facing each other to create a nice, clean "lane" to the fireplace.

DAVE: *I don't know if I like that you call them "dueling" sofas.*

KORTNEY: *It's a design term.*

DAVE: *I don't love it.*

KORTNEY: *Do you want to fight about it?*

DAVE: *Yes, we can fight about it from our dueling sofas.*

KORTNEY: *Touché.*

Okay, so let's imagine ourselves sitting comfortably across from one another on our *harmonious, not-in-the-least-bit-argumentative* matching sofas. What might we see in our fireplace?

Fire-Free Fireplace Options

- **Candles in a variety of heights and sizes** are a popular choice for obvious reasons. While you can never go wrong with a classic layering of white on white, I like to choose one of the room's accent colors and select a variety of candles in varying shades or values of that color. Say your room is primarily white, with gray and fuchsia accents; decorating with candles in a variety of purples and pinks will literally bring your accent color to light—and the color variations will keep it from looking too matchy-matchy. Set the candles in glass holders for a more formal look, or use a bed of black or white decor stones to finesse it up a bit. The candles should really be at varying heights, or it will look like you bought a box set of candles and set them on the ground. Have some fun with it instead! When I say "varying heights," I mean *really* varying heights. Some can sit on books, so the candle is as tall as the opening. Others can be wide and low. Mixing candle sticks and tea lights is perfectly acceptable too. Just give it a human touch.

- **Vases are also "lit."** To borrow a phrase from my son Jett's generation, varied vases are "totally lit." (That's a good thing. Apparently.) As always, vary up the heights, and resist the urge to put flowers or plants in all of them. One or two will be *perfect*.

- **Framed photos** can absolutely work, but you have to be mindful to ensure it says "fun" and not "funeral." Unless you really are memorializing the person, a framed photo of a family member with a candle beside it (resting in a fireplace!) can look one Ouija board shy of a séance. If you want to go the framed photo route, treat the fireplace like a console table and leave the candles out of the equation. Consider building a shelf into the space to get your accent pieces off the ground, then apply the rule of threes to stage it. A stack of books, framed photo on top, sweet succulent to the side, and you're good to go.

- **Keep it contained.** Whatever you decide to put in your fireplace, make sure it doesn't protrude beyond the opening. It's okay if objects flank or frame the fireplace, but having something oversize, like a massive fern—or your great-grandmother's antique suitcase—spilling out of the hearth will appear at best unbalanced and at worst like your fireplace is vomiting into the living area.

- **Why not wallpaper or paint?** While I wouldn't suggest wallpapering the *actual* inside of the fireplace, you could easily apply a cool wallpaper print to a plywood board and set it inside the fireplace as a backdrop. Alternatively, you could paint the interior a bright jewel tone that plays nicely with your room's color palette.

- **Tile and smile.** A fun patterned tile on the exterior and hearth can be a gorgeous focal point in a room that's generally more muted. Add an antique standing mirror the width and height of the opening for added romance. It will reflect the light in the room and draw attention to your masterpiece.

- **Don't be a basket case.** I love decorative baskets tucked inside a fireplace, but it's a look that begs to be multiplied. One basket in a fireplace says "sacrificial offering; someone get me a match," whereas multiple baskets, filled with spare blankets and pillows, says "cozy cluster of style." A fireplace is, by nature, solid, sturdy, and grounded. It also extends to the height of the house (whether you see it or not), so you can't do anything dinky in there—or your design will be swallowed whole.

- **The combo.** This move is not for amateurs—but you're an expert by now, right? Try creating varied stacks of colorful old books (find them—or paint them!) and top some with complementary colored vases and others with candles. Throw in one of Grandma's tchotchkes for good measure, and you've got yourself a fireplace *and* a conversation piece.

MAKE SPACE
FOR ROUTINES

———

If someone had predicted that I would become a full-time working mom who homeschooled her three kids, I would have told them to stop sniffing the rubber cement. I've been called a lot of things in my life, but "teacher" was definitely not one of them. That is, until my boys hit middle school.

Here in Nashville, middle school starts in fifth grade, and because of the way our public schools are structured, not every child is guaranteed a spot at their first-choice school (or even their second- or third-choice school, for that matter). It's all based on a lottery system—and until selection day, there's no telling where in the city your kids will land. When you multiply those odds (and logistics) by two or more children, homeschooling can start to look easy by comparison. In fact, it's so common in our community for kids to be homeschooled—and so socially supported—I often forget it's not the norm.

When we failed to win a spot at our school of choice, Dave and I weighed all of our options and decided to take a leap of faith and put on our teacher hats.

DAVE: *And within a week and a half, I realized the teacher hat didn't fit nearly as well as any of my other hats.*

KORTNEY: *No.*

DAVE: *It also didn't go with anything in my closet.*

KORTNEY: *So instead of buying yourself a whole new wardrobe . . .*

DAVE: *I just gave you my hat.*

KORTNEY: *You've always been a giver.*

DAVE: *Not to mention a problem solver. Plus, you look super cute in my hat.*

Honestly, I kind of predicted the bulk of the teaching would fall to me, and I embraced it, right along with the opportunity to design the space that would become our homeschool classroom. While I've always been a fan of routines, homeschooling took our reliance on them to a whole new level, and I became acutely aware of the role design plays in creating a space that supports (or hinders) successful routines.

Generally speaking, I approach design the way I would a math problem: What is the problem we are trying to solve? What are the knowns? What are the unknowns? What formulas will we use to solve it? When designing your space around a particular routine, it's the same idea—but with a lot more variables. So you have to break it down. Swallow that elephant one bite at a time.

What Is the Question Your Space Needs to Answer?

For us, the big question was, *How do we create a space that's conducive to learning?* I really wanted this to be an inspiring space for the kids. Waving a wand over the kitchen table and calling it a classroom was not going to cut it. To get our guys geared up for learning at home, I needed them to know that this endeavor was new, it was different, and it was going to be *awesome*.

Which meant I needed *a space* that was new, different, and awesome.

Awesome new spaces are not easy to come by in an old house you're already living in, so a bit of creativity was in order.

We had a little nook under the staircase, with its own side entrance that we hardly used, and it quickly dawned on me that this underutilized and out-of-the-way space had great potential

to become a place for quiet study. I bought a piece of inexpensive butcher block ($20) so the kids had a desk to work on. I painted the main walls a clean white to eliminate distractions and added one chartreuse accent wall to give it some life. Dave brought in some cool black rolling chairs—something the kids would never have in *regular* school—and *voilà*: something new, something different, something *awesome*.

What Does Your Routine Actually Look Like?

You'd be surprised how many people design for the destination but not the journey. The routine is the journey, and if it's one you plan to take every day, be sure to take a good, hard look at it *before* you design your space. Write it down. Draw it out on a piece of paper. Whatever you need to do to visualize the routine, do it. Then make your design decisions accordingly. I knew we'd be taking a structured approach to homeschooling, and before I designed the space, I thought about what I wanted a typical day to look like. We start at eight in the morning and end at three in the afternoon, just like regular school, but we have more breaks throughout the day, and there's no homework so long as everyone stays focused.

The nook is great for independent study, but we also needed a common area where we could all sit and learn together. Since the study nook is attached to our playroom, we use that as a classroom during the day. We have a round

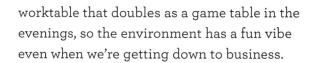

worktable that doubles as a game table in the evenings, so the environment has a fun vibe even when we're getting down to business.

Separate Routines from the Rest of It

Few people have the luxury of dedicating an entire space to just one activity, but that's completely okay as long as you're deliberate about separating one routine from the rest. Since our playroom doubles as a classroom, I bought some inexpensive six-drawer dressers *just for school* and labeled the drawers by class, so the kids could keep their work separate from each other and out of the way.

Three years later, I still love walking into this space, sitting down with a kid and a cup of tea, and teaching a math lesson—something I never thought I'd say.

LOVE YOUR LINENS

———

Have you ever stopped to consider how much time you actually spend in your bedroom? If you're doing it right, sleep alone should account for one-third of your life; so why do so many people treat their bedroom like an afterthought?

DAVE: *Because when they're sleeping, they're unconscious?*

KORTNEY: *That's no excuse.*

DAVE: *You're scary.*

KORTNEY: *So are ugly bedrooms.*

DAVE: *I know you are, but what am I?*

KORTNEY: *WHAT?*

DAVE: *I don't know. I got caught up in the moment and kind of lost the thread there.*

To Dave's point, so many people neglect the design of their bedrooms because they figure that room is for their eyes only.

DAVE: *Or not even for their eyes. Since their eyes are closed.*

KORTNEY: *Let it go, honey.*

I went to visit my sister and brother-in-law last winter, and she asked me to help her shop for one room in the house, my pick. I immediately zeroed in on the bedroom. Why? Because it's the place where we begin and end our days. It sets the tone for our mornings and it's the last thing we see before we close our eyes at night. If the bed linens are beautiful and inviting, you will feel better and sleep better. I promise you.

Over the next 24 hours, my sister and I shopped until we dropped. I had decided to do a complete room makeover, with new paint, new lighting, new curtains—the works. While she put her trust in me, she questioned nearly every decision I made. And when I started to stock up on new bedding (an extra duvet, extra blankets, and some cozy pillows), she started to panic. She just couldn't see the need for this "extravagance" and was certain her husband wouldn't either.

DAVE: *Let me guess who won that battle.*

KORTNEY: *It's futile to resist me.*

When I revealed the room to her, she *cried*. She couldn't believe how warm and inviting and *comfortable* the room looked. What had been a place to turn off the lights and crash after a long day was now an oasis they were excited to retreat to. And despite her objections, she could not deny that the quality linens and "extra" bedding played a huge part in the transformation.

My Lean on Linens

- **White linens win.** Lord knows I love color, but I am all about white linens. We have dogs and kids. And none of us is opposed to breakfast (or dinner and a movie) in bed. When there are spills, I bleach them out, and my fabulous white linens are as good as new.

- **Thread count counts.** So do online reviews. I don't spend too much time contemplating thread counts and cotton types, but I do look at online reviews. Those usually result in me buying sheets that are at least 400 thread count and either Egyptian or Pima cotton, but not always. My favorite sheets of all time I purchased online for $30. That's a *steal* for a king-size set, and I'll admit I was nervous that the price was so low. But the

reviews don't lie (at least, not *all* of them), and 50 million Elvis fans can't be wrong.

- **Consider your body temperature.** If you run hot, choose fibers that breathe really beautifully. Bamboo sheets, for example, are super soft and breathable—and eco-friendly to boot. Flannel sheets, while not my personal favorite, are beloved by the cold-blooded members of our family.

- **How much do you hate wrinkles?** If you're completely type A and feel the need to iron your sheets, there are wrinkle-free fabrics that are serious time savers. Keep in mind, though, that these sheets are treated with chemicals to make them that way, so if you're all about organics, this option may not appeal to you. Pulling your sheets out of the dryer and folding them while they're still warm is my go-to move to reduce wrinkles and not have to iron.

- **Soft and durable?** Not likely. For me, the softer the sheets, the better. I'm less concerned that they'll last a lifetime (which the super-softest sheets tend *not* to do) and I'm more interested in the short game (SLEEP, GLORIOUS SLEEP). Sateen or Egyptian cottons are my favorites.

- **Double up.** There's nothing like climbing into a bed with freshly cleaned sheets, but I *hate* having to change the sheets if it means not making the bed in the morning. If an unmade bed makes you lose your head, do as I do and buy two sets of linens (*and duvet covers*). They don't have to be identical—in fact, I kind of like to change it up and enjoy a slightly different vibe while my other sheets are out of rotation.

- **Cover your coverlet.** The duvet cover is an absolute *must* for me. A duvet without a cover is like a pillow without a case.

DAVE: *And remind me: Is a pillow without a case a felony, or just a misdemeanor?*

KORTNEY: *It may not be against the law, but it is criminal, and I will issue you a citation.*

DAVE: *I think you're flirting with me, officer.*

Tuck in the top sheet. It drives me bananas when people leave the flat sheet untucked. The corners should be folded under the mattress neatly, not flapping in the breeze like racing flags. That way when you crawl into bed at night, you're crawling *in*, not under.

Face down with the flat sheet. This is a subject of some debate, not unlike the great "over or under" argument people have about toilet paper. I fall squarely in the camp of facedown flat sheets, so when you fold them over your accent blanket, the pretty side faces up. If your duvet covers the whole bed and the sheets don't show, I'll give you a pass on this final point. I'm not *that* much of a stickler.

DAVE: *Yes, she is.*

KORTNEY: *Yes, I am.*

IF YOU'RE GOING TO PLAY BALL, YOU'VE GOTTA HAVE A SIGN

One of the secrets to a happy marriage is the ability to let the little things go. Dave and I are firm believers in getting over minor disagreements as quickly as humanly possible. Especially those petty little arguments that don't amount to anything more than a bad mood and a wasted hour for both of us.

DAVE: *Like the time you got mad at me for forgetting to take Lennox to gymnastics.*

KORTNEY: *Okay, it was way more than one time. Which is why I got so ticked.*

DAVE: *Fine. Maybe it was two times.*

KORTNEY: *It was slightly less than* all *the times, but a lot more than two.*

DAVE: *Fine. I have a bag of Cheese Nips for brains. That is a well-established fact of our marriage. So rather than fighting about it, this is when we do the sign.*

Exactly. When an argument starts to escalate (as above), and we just know it's not worth the effort, we both do the sign—and the fight is declared over.

DAVE: *And we delete the fight from the marriage database without having to utter those pesky little words "I'm sorry."*

YOU CAN NEVER HAVE TOO MANY BLANKETS

I am a sucker for a cute blanket. It's a passion that borders on obsession, and no matter how hard I try to control myself, I can't resist the siren song of a soft, colorful throw in the season's hottest color. Throw blankets are a designer's dream accessory. They're soft, colorful, portable, and practical—and they can even save you money in the winter months, when heating bills are at an all-time high. They're also one of the most affordable, risk-free ways to add color and texture to a room.

How I Make the Most of My (Never Too Many) Blankets

- **Stack 'em.** Like hardbound books, only softer! I love to see a stack of colorful blankets tucked in tight on a high shelf.

- **Over, under.** The beauty of blankets (other than the obvious) is how versatile they are. Tossed, draped, folded, or stacked, they look lovely. If you want to be sure they stay in place (rather than ending up on the floor),

try draping them over the back of your couch or chair, and under the seat cushion.

- **Try two or more.** I love to pair two blankets in complementary colors (and similar or identical textures) and drape them side by side, or slightly overlapping, over a soft seat back. This is a great way to repeat one of the room's accent colors—and temper it with another color to keep the whole space from being too matchy-matchy.

- **Accent an ottoman.** Ottomans make great coffee tables. And blankets make ottomans come to life. Fold a bold-print blanket lengthwise, drape it over the ottoman, and put a pretty tray on top for candles and coffee cups.

- **Basket of blankets.** Nothing says "nestle in" like a pretty basket of blankets beside a sofa or reading chair. I use the blanket basket in staging all the time, because it looks pretty and feels no-fuss. Ideally all of the blankets would be complementary colors, with one or two draped elegantly over the basket's edge—but honestly a basket of mismatched blankets is better than a room draped with mismatched blankets—and that's the key here. *Keep those beauties contained.*

- **On a ladder.** I love a rustic blanket ladder draped with pretty throws and juxtaposed with more sleek and modern decor, which tends to have a cooler vibe. This is a great place to go crazy with color, since the ladder's rungs make a natural visual organizer. Try draping a spectrum of complementary tones (red, orange, and yellow, or chartreuse, green, and blue) to make a neutral space feel bold and vibrant.

- **Impromptu picnics.** Indoors or out, there's something about a picnic blanket that says "instant party." I love tossing a blanket and pillows on the floor, laying out the snacks, and settling in for family movie night.

- **Blanket forts, duh.** What's more fun than family movie night? Family movie night in an epic blanket fort, of course. Let the kids cozy up and get creative. This is one time where neatness is not required. Layer up all the blankets you can find and hide away for awhile.

DAVE: *This last tip is recommended for recreational home use only. Blanket forts in the workplace are generally frowned upon. Don't ask me how I know.*

KORTNEY: *That was you who left the afghan and Ho Ho wrappers under our desk? I made Jett and Sully clean that up. I'm impressed that they didn't rat you out.*

DAVE: *Every man knows the first rule of Blanket Fort Club is, you do not talk about Blanket Fort Club.*

KORTNEY: *Well, tell the "Blanket Fort Club" I have your flashlight.*

BREAK THIS WINDOW RULE

There are some design rules that become so ingrained in the public psyche, it's almost impossible to convince people to break them. "Thou shalt not put beds in front of windows" is one such commandment, and for the life of me, I can't see why.

DAVE: *Maybe it's because you're in bed and your back is to the window.*

KORTNEY: *Are the window commandments posted outside in our yard?*

DAVE: *YOU'LL NEVER KNOW.*

Well, I've never lost sleep over placing a bed in front of a window. In fact, I've embraced it. Unless you're building a house from the ground up, you're at the mercy of the current layout, so you might as well make the windows work for you. Wherever they are. When I list houses for my clients, I'm amazed at the lengths they will go to avoid putting a bed in front of a window, even if it means sticking the bed in a corner or against a wall that the door opens into, disrupting traffic flow. These are far worse transgressions, in my opinion, and yet that window rule reigns supreme in their minds. I would love it if every bed faced a window that revealed goats grazing merrily in a lavender meadow outside. I would also love it if the sun could rise and set on the same side of the house for my viewing pleasure, but that's probably not going to happen.

DAVE: *Um, that's* definitely *not going to happen.*

KORTNEY: *Well, I'm a rule breaker and an optimist. What can I say.*

DAVE: *You may be a rule breaker, but you are definitely not an optimist.*

KORTNEY: *You're right. I'm a realist. And there are a lot of wonky windows in our future, so let's continue.*

Wonky-Window Solutions

- **Keep a low profile.** If the bed must go in front of the window and the window is in the middle of the wall, choose a low-profile bed and let the window act as the headboard.

- **Frame the window** with some paneled curtains and hang them high and wide. The goal isn't to cover the windows (blinds will do the trick for that). Layer on the coordinating bed linens to complete the look.

- **Own it, don't hide it.** Stay away from four-poster beds and beds with canopies. The window is now part of the bed design, so you don't want to cover it up.

- **Curtains can serve as a headboard.** If you have a wall of windows, you can center the bed and hang curtains behind it. The windows on either side of the bed will let the light in and the panels (hung as high as possible, of course) will act as a dramatic headboard. You can also do this curtain "headboard" in front of a smaller window, obscuring the window entirely *if* (and only if) the room has a ton of natural light coming in from other sources.

- **No symmetry, no problem.** Do you have to put a bed on a wall with an off-center window? Place the bed in the middle of the wall and balance the window on one side with a similarly sized mirror or art on the other. An oversize chandelier in the center of the room can serve as a strong focal point to distract from the asymmetrical backdrop and to balance the space further.

Where Else Can I Break the Rules?

The bedroom's not the only place people get hamstrung by hard-and-fast window rules. They'll go to great lengths, including *not having* a freestanding tub, just to ensure the tub's not beside a window. But I don't think this setup is a design flaw at all. I deliberately design our houses to accommodate natural light behind freestanding tubs. You can shutter or tint the window, so you don't become the talk of the town, and still enjoy the view. There's nothing like moonlight and candlelight to complete your moment of serenity at the end of the day. The all-in-one tub/shower enclosure is a different story. Showering in front of a window is

less than serene (for most of us anyway), and I would consider removing the window altogether if possible. If that can't happen, glass blocks or tinted tempered glass can also work, but it's never ideal.

DAVE: *So, to recap: sleeping in front of a window is fine, bathing in front of a window is magical, and showering in front of a window is . . .*

KORTNEY: *A felony.*

DAVE: *Only if you get caught doing it more than once. Otherwise I think it's just a misdemeanor.*

KORTNEY: *I'm not going to ask why you've researched this.*

DAVE: *This conversation is not intended to convey or constitute legal advice and is not a substitute for obtaining legal advice from a qualified attorney. But showering in front of a window is definitely creepy and might get you arrested.*

KORTNEY: *Thanks, Dave.*

DON'T SAY "CHEESE!"

I am the crazy camera lady. I *love* taking pictures, and there's nothing anyone can do or say to stop me. You can shame me all day long for not simply *"being* in the moment," but guess who has an awesome slideshow of that moment? NOT YOU! Me. Mwahahaha.

If you don't love taking photos, don't worry about it. But if you do? Don't apologize. Just keep shooting. Your family and friends will thank you when your handiwork pops up in their Facebook memories next year.

Pointers for Shutterbugs

Don't say cheese. Here's what happens when you tell a group of kids to say cheese:

Where are their eyes? Covered in "cheese," that's where. Instead, ask them to say a word that naturally relaxes the face muscles.

DAVE: *Like "whiskey"?*

KORTNEY: *I was thinking something more kid appropriate—like "money."*

DAVE: *What kind of kids are you raising?*

KORTNEY: *Well, it works.*

Capture candids. Some of my favorite family photos are the ones we didn't plan or stage. The kids walking together in a line. Snap. Dave fast asleep in bed, with our dog Donnie tucked in and snoring beside him. Snap. I recently took a photo of Dave at his mother's memorial, and I'll admit I questioned whether maybe I'd finally lost my marbles taking pictures in that moment. But I wanted to capture the essence of this day, celebrating and remembering Dave's mom.

DAVE: *Are you talking about the picture of me laying my mother's ashes to rest?*

KORTNEY: *Okay. When you say it like that, you make me sound like a callous paparazzo.*

DAVE: *[silence]*

KORTNEY: *IT WAS A BEAUTIFUL MOMENT. I couldn't help myself.*

Dave had just laid the ashes to rest and he was looking up at our son Sully. The glance between them in that moment spoke volumes. *This is weird, right? Do we cry or make a joke? Grandma would make a joke. I'm happy she's*

at peace. *Finally.* All of that, in one picture. I couldn't resist.

Buy a ring light. If you like taking portraits, a ring light is a (relatively) inexpensive way to take your photography to the next level. This super simple ring-shaped light will cast a gorgeous light on your subject's eyes and emit an even light over the face to help eliminate shadows.

Have a sense of humor. Let's say you're staging a family photo and one of your kids decides this is the perfect moment to spontaneously combust. Own it, and go with the flow. Instruct the rest of your brood to fake cry along with him and make it your next Christmas card. This is the stuff memories are made of.

Dress for success. The best photos are the ones where everyone is comfortable and feeling their best. When people are relaxed, they're more likely to let loose and look like themselves. If your six grown sons have never worn suits a day in their lives, now is not the time to start. Best to wear what comes naturally.

Find an inspiration photo. Professionals do it, and you can too. Search the web for some fun reference photos that you all love and use that as your guide. When everyone has some general direction, the fun stuff tends to follow.

No uniforms. I'm not a fan of family photos where everyone wears the same outfit. Unless it's a wedding and you're the bride, you don't need to dictate that everyone dress alike. Instead, think in broad strokes. Palette, not paint color. You might, for example, tell everyone to choose shades of blue and green and avoid patterns and big logos, but be warned that if you send out a memo that says "Everyone wear red," your family photo will look at worst like a crime scene and at best like an employee picnic.

Did I Say No Uniforms? There Are a Few Exceptions

Respect your elders. If you've finally gathered the entire extended family for a family reunion at the beach and Grandma decides you're all going to have your picture taken wearing white shirts and khakis and bare feet, *you are all going to have your picture taken wearing white shirts and khakis and bare feet. And you are going to LIKE it.* Don't mess with Grandma.

Matching Christmas PJ's. Ho, ho, ho yes, my friends. This is one time of year when everyone wearing polka-dot pj's with bum flaps may never go out of style. I may even have one or two of these in our family album.

   DAVE: *Eleven. You have eleven of them.*

They are cheesy and ridiculous and *adorable.*

Disney World. Permission to wear matching mouse ears? GRANTED.

KIDS SAY THE DARNDEST THINGS . . . WRITE THEM DOWN

You think you'll remember, but you won't. When our first child, Jett, was three, he started saying the heart-meltingest things, like a tiny, blond-haired, blue-eyed Hallmark card. "No matter how old I get, Mommy," he once said, "I'll always be your little boy." Unforgettable, right? WRONG. The only reason I remember that one is because I wrote it down.

For every precious phrase I dutifully recorded, there are 10 more I'll never get back. That's why, when our next child, the quotable Sully Wilson, came along, I started the online document called "Our Kids Say the Darndest Things." And it might be the best gift I've ever given myself.

Every year on their birthdays, I pull out a few of their one-liners to share. (I figure this will be good preparation for their wedding days, when I project my all-time favorites onto the big screen beside their bath-time baby photos.)

You never know when the verbal gems are coming, so the key is to jot down the quotes as soon as they're spoken. I use an app on my phone and keep the whole list online and accessible wherever I go. If I wait even 24 hours, the treasured moments might be lost forever.

DAVE: *And I would have way more self-esteem than I do now.*

A FEW OF OUR GREATEST HITS

JETT: *Mom, is it hard to cook?*

KORTNEY: *No, but sometimes you have to make bad stuff to learn what works and what doesn't.*

JETT: *Daddy's been in that phase for a while.*

SULLY: *Dad, do you love one kid more than the others?*

DAVE: *I love different things about each of my kids, because each of you is unique and special. But I couldn't love one of you more than the others—my love for you will always be equal.*

SULLY: *I love Mommy more than I love you.*

—

DAVE *(whispers into Lennox's ear): Lennox, you are such a smart girl.*

LENNOX *(whispers back): And you are a fat guy.*

CLEAN YOUR ENTIRE HOUSE IN 20 MINUTES A DAY

There are people who *sashay* through clutter like RuPaul on a rubbish runway. They know the kids are just having fun! They know that mess will get cleaned up . . . *eventually*. And if it doesn't, well, at least there's a half pack of uneaten airline peanuts under the couch cushions to munch on while they wait out the storm.

I love those people.

I *salute* those people.

But I am *not* one of those people.

Our home is not a museum by any means. All day long, kids and dogs and friends come and go. And come and go. And come. And go. The only visitors who take their shoes off are the Canadians (it's just not a tradition here), so there's a fair amount of . . . earthly matter . . . making its way through our revolving door. I welcome the hustle and bustle with open arms, but at the end of the day, when it's just us Wilsons, I've been known to cry "ALL HANDS ON DECK" for the 20-minute power clean.

Full disclosure: we do have an amazing woman who gives our home a deep clean every couple of weeks, and she is a lifesaver. It's during the meantime, the in-between time, that our 20-minute magic routine keeps things tidy—in the house, and in my head.

If you survey your family (and be sure to give them multiple-choice questions), you will find that certain family members gravitate toward certain jobs. I'll vacuum the main floor, Sully will vacuum upstairs, Jett will take on all countertops with a surprising vengeance, and Dave will eagerly sign up for sinks and toilets (because he's a total weirdo). Younger kids will grow into the jobs that require a bit more elbow grease, but they're usually pretty willing to pick up their toys and put away all of the little things that have been left around. (And it's usually their toys and little things that have been left around, so . . . more than fair.)

Once jobs are assigned, we blare music until we can't hear ourselves think (or whine). We set the timer (even though we can't hear it go off) and clean as fast as we possibly can to beat the clock. We reconvene in the kitchen for a fun snack and I get to breathe easy again.

DAVE WILSON MASTER CLASS
DO THE "DAD CLEAN"

Every time Kortney goes out of town, our house turns on me like a scorned lover. Dust and dirty laundry and bowls of half-eaten cereal appear within 14 seconds of her walking out the door. And that's *before* the kids get home from their sleepovers and sports practices. Once the kids are back in the mix, all bets are off. I'm basically clawing my way out of a ball pit until Kortney comes home.

> **KORTNEY:** *I didn't know you felt this way. I thought you were pretty zen about single-dadding.*

> **DAVE:** *Zen? No. But I do have a two-word mantra that I chant to keep myself centered.*

> **KORTNEY:** *What is it?*

> **DAVE:** *Damage. Control.*

The most intense stretch of Kortney's absences is always the 24 hours before she gets back. For that I've developed the Dave Wilson Dad Clean System (patent pending). And now, for a limited time only, this five- or six-dollar value is yours at no additional cost when you purchase this book (which you already have, so congratulations).

The Dave Wilson Dad Clean System

MIDNIGHT BEFORE

At midnight, before Kortney returns, I run the Roomba robot vacuum. We named her Judy, after the Jetsons. Several people have already pointed out that the Jetsons' robot was actually named Rosie, and what can I say? We're idiots. But Judy doesn't let that stop her. She's a total boss at cleaning the floors.

About three hours prior to reentry (Kortney's), I stand in the middle of the kitchen and scream "INCOMING! INCOMING!" Everyone gets on all fours with a cloth and dusts the stairs, because Judy doesn't do stairs.

MIDMORNING

I throw a splash of Ajax in the toilets and sinks. You don't actually have to clean them. You can fake them all except for the kitchen sink.

KORTNEY: *Do you seriously do that?*

DAVE: *No!*

DAVE: *(Yes.)*

I hand each kid three Clorox wipes and say, "Go! Wipe three things."

36 MINUTES PRIOR TO THE EAGLE LANDING

1. Sauté a chopped onion in olive oil.

2. Let "home cooked" aroma permeate kitchen for 20 minutes.

3. Proceed to make pasta with cheap store-bought tomato sauce.

4. Discard onion.

Welcome home, baby. You hungry?

YOU'VE GOT TO HAVE YOUR GIRLS

I didn't have a lot of girlfriends growing up. Girls can be cruel in middle and high school, and those were particularly difficult years for me. To this day, I keep in touch with more friends from elementary school than I do from the upper grades. I went to a performing arts high school for two years, but even among my peers who loved the same things I did, I just never fit in. I knew I wanted to pursue a career in music, and 100 percent of my attention was focused on that goal.

DAVE: *Boooo. What about boys? And partying? And high-waisted jeans? Where were your priorities?*

KORTNEY: *Exactly. My priorities were completely out of whack as far as my friends were concerned.*

I had three friends in 10th grade I considered close. But when I decided to finish my last two years of high school via correspondence so I could pursue music and theater professionally, they stopped speaking to me. It was the loneliest time in my life, but I used the loneliness to drive me. In fact, that loneliness drove me all the way to Nashville.

DAVE: *I thought your mom drove you to Nashville in a Datsun hatchback?*

KORTNEY: *It was a minivan, actually. And she was behind the wheel, but loneliness was straddling the emergency brake between us for sure.*

Because of the popularity awards I *didn't* win back in the day, I place enormous value on the female friendships I have now. I am lucky to be married to my best friend in the world, and man, does he have my back, but there's just no substitute for female friendships. There are so many women in my life now who show up for me with strength and encouragement and unconditional love, I'm almost grateful for the time when this wasn't the case, because I appreciate my friendships that much more.

I think Dave values those friendships as much as I do. When life comes at me with a fistful of garbage, and I don't have the energy to duck, Dave will call in the troops on my behalf. I've had friends show up at my door with instructions from Dave to take me to our neighborhood restaurant. And when we got there, our menus were whisked away and the chef brought us a specially prepared meal with specialty drink pairings, all masterminded and paid for in advance by Dave.

He knows that I will leave with a depleted heart and return home filled to the brim—with food, and drink, and the unconditional love of friends.

DAVE: *And at least one disgusting R-rated story you'll laugh yourself to sleep over.*

KORTNEY: *At* least *one.*

MAKE A SCENE!

—

It was Garth Brooks who sparked my love of country music.

DAVE: *It was also Garth Brooks who sparked your love of Garth Brooks.*

KORTNEY: *The man, the myth, the legend.*

DAVE: *The tight jeans, the cowboy boots . . .*

KORTNEY: *And his hats. I love the way that man looks in a cowboy hat. To this day, it gets me right here.*

DAVE: *I'm not going to tell you where she's pointing.*

When I heard Garth was coming to Nashville on tour last year, I literally pounced on a pair of tickets. The first and last time I'd seen him perform live was on his second world tour in 1998, shortly after I moved to Nashville. I was basically ready to relive my youth, this time with Dave by my side.

We decided to make a big night of it, dressing up like true-blue country fans. Dave wore his tightest jeans, belt buckle, boots, and an old cowboy hat he'd saved from back in the day. I'd never seen him in jeans that tight.

DAVE: *I intimidated myself, those jeans were so tight.*

KORTNEY: *We both looked like three pounds of meat in a two-pound bag. But it was GARTH. We had to do it right.*

We ate dinner at The Palm, which is a pretty high-end restaurant across the street from the venue, and the two of us stuck out like two sore thumbs with our ridiculous outfits. We didn't care.

DAVE: *Because GARTH!*

But when we got inside the arena—where the show was completely sold out, by the way—we were the *only ones* dressed up in country garb.

DAVE: *Literally. Not a cowboy hat or pair of boots in sight. Just millennials in base-ball caps for miles. And Dave and Kortney looking like an episode of* Hee Haw.

People kept coming up to us and saying, "I love your costumes." It was hilarious, and we didn't care one bit.

DAVE: *We knew Garth would understand.*

Except that when Garth took the stage, even *he* was wearing baggy jeans and a ball cap. Even his merchandise crew weren't selling cowboy hats. Just ball caps.

DAVE: *Like the ones Garth Brooks wears.*

I genuinely thought we were dressing the part that night. And I can't believe it never occurred to me that maybe, just maybe, the cowboy trend had shifted in the two *decades* since I'd seen him last. Considering all the trends that have shifted since last *season,* you'd think I might have seen the possibility.

DAVE: *You know what they say. Love is blind.*

KORTNEY: *And I will never forget that concert as long as I live.*

DAVE: *And that concert probably won't forget us either.*

Sometimes when you try to make the scene, you end up making *a* scene instead. Own it! Part of life is being comfortable in your own skin. Even when you're wearing a ridiculous hat and your jeans are way too tight.

That's how memories are made.

STAY SAFE

When our first son, Jett, was born, the carefree spirit who once lived inside me was suddenly replaced with a throbbing worry-wart. There I was, married to the man of my dreams; we'd bought a house, we had big plans, our gorgeous baby boy was healthy and thriving. Life was good.

Too good.

I was convinced something terrible was going to happen, which sent me down a rabbit hole hunting for ways to protect our little family.

Two more children later, most of my semi-hysterical safety measures have fallen by the wayside. But one precautionary practice remains.

Inside our kitchen pantry and behind every medicine cabinet, I keep a laminated "Steps to Safety" card, which lists the latest phone numbers and best practices for common emergencies. Do I smother a stove fire—or throw water on it? I can never remember. And I don't have to, because I keep that info in arm's reach. CPR is another one that changes from time to time, and while I have the best intentions of taking the classes every year, it gives me peace of mind to know that the steps are there if I—or any one of us—needs them.

DAVE: *Tell them about the Davey-Do List.*

KORTNEY: *I don't call it that.*

DAVE: *You might as well.*

I do keep a laminated home safety calendar that reminds me to change the batteries in the smoke detectors, test the GFCIs, and replace the air filters.

DAVE: *It reminds "you" to do it?*

KORTNEY: *Well, it reminds me to tell you to do it, which is basically the same thing.*

DAVE: *Only better!*

KORTNEY: *You at least get the satisfaction of checking the little box with a dry-erase marker every time you complete a task.*

DAVE: *I'm supposed to check a little box?*

KORTNEY: *It's the most satisfying part!*

While all of this may sound obvious and basic, I'm surprised how many people don't do it. In a day and age when peace of mind doesn't come easy, this one seems like a no-brainer.

Consider keeping the following on hand:

- Fire safety instructions
- CPR instructions
- Emergency phone numbers
- Smoke detector batteries—change date
- Air filters—change date
- Carbon monoxide detector battery—change date
- Special emergency instructions for your family's specific health concerns, such as allergies

A friend of mine who has a severe allergy to shellfish has a letter to her elementary school-age son taped to the back of their front door, explaining what it might look like if she was experiencing an allergic reaction and giving him instructions for what to do and who to call. I was touched by the way she wrote directly to him, acknowledging the fear he might feel in the moment and encouraging him to act on her behalf, as she would if she were present in the moment. That's what these lists mean to me. Utilitarian as they may seem—and easy as they are to push aside for another day—they really are an expression of love and caring for everyone in the home.

REDEFINE
DATE NIGHT

———

I admire couples who do date night religiously once a week. I also understand my friend who says, "I got married so I could stop dating. The last thing I want to do is date my wife." But whether or not you *call it* "date night," I'm a firm believer that couples have to carve out time alone together to nurture their relationship, and they have to do it often.

This can be tricky for Dave and me, because we work together. Sometimes more togetherness is the last thing we think we need. But we still need it. What's important is *not* that it looks like a date. What's important is that whatever we choose to do looks *different* from our day-to-day routine. It doesn't have to be fancy, but it does have to be an escape.

I've seen couples put too much pressure on date night being "special" or "romantic" or "new and exciting." That's not us. At least, not right now. These days, we're more likely to be found under the covers binge-watching Netflix with a couple of containers of Chinese takeout and a "No Talking about Work" policy firmly in place.

LET DESTINY DO HER THING

On our first date, I told Dave that I wanted to adopt a child someday. "If that's a deal breaker for you," I said, "tell me now."

DAVE: *I don't think anything would have been a deal breaker for me. You could have told me you wanted to live on Mars and start a wild hamster circus, and I would have been like, "Sounds amazing." It was a pretty good first date.*

It *was* a good first date, but I still don't think he knew how serious I was about adoption. For whatever reason, I had always felt like it was meant to be part of my story.

Shortly after Sully was born, I printed out the paperwork to begin the adoption process, knowing that it might take a year or more to find a match. Dave wasn't ready, but that came as no surprise. Dave's never ready. He hadn't been ready for Jett and he hadn't been ready to start trying for a second. And yet, here we were. Parents of two. Sometimes you just need your partner to pull you along. And as soon as the ball was rolling, Dave was all in and ready to meet our new baby.

Adoption is not for the faint of heart. The road is long and unpredictable and fraught with unknowns. Our own journey began with a painful failed adoption that brought us to our knees. It took about 12 weeks to find a match, and when we finally did, Dave and I were ecstatic. After four months of classes and meetings, doctors appointments, fingerprints, interviews, and a home study, we drove six hours to Mississippi to meet the birth father and mother at a neighborhood Applebee's.

As we were crossing county lines, they called us, wanting to cancel our meeting because their car was out of gas. It was a red flag to me, but this was simply their reality. We asked them to meet us at a gas station, which was as far as they could drive with the little gas they had. Dave and I filled up their tank and we went ahead with the meeting, which felt strained, awkward, uncomfortable, and exciting all at the same time. I kept wanting to explain to our server why we were all there, convinced everyone in the room felt as awkward as I did. I wanted so badly to be myself, but I felt like I was being interviewed (which I was). I'm sure they did too. As the night went

on, we were able to find some common ground. The couple had four children already—four boys—and Dave and I had two. We talked about the challenges of parenting. We tried to get to know each other. The mother was only 21 years old and I kept looking at her, thinking, *I can't believe I'm sitting with the mother of my baby.*

Not wanting to get our hopes up, we asked if they had any family members who might want to care for this baby, and they said no. No family members had supported the other four, and this child would be no exception. They had made up their minds that adoption was the right thing for this child, a baby girl.

So we let our hearts believe. We decorated our baby's nursery and hung up her tiny clothes. We let ourselves imagine our lives as a family of five. She was our girl.

And then she wasn't.

The day before her mother gave birth, our attorney called to tell us that the family had had a change of heart. The baby's paternal grand-parents had decided they would support the child after all.

Dave and I were heartbroken and stunned. I literally fell to the floor, where I spent much of the following days in the fetal position, not eating, not sleeping, just crying over the loss of a child who was never mine.

Maybe you've picked up on this, but I am not one to waver. I knew adoption was woven into my destiny, but this loss had rocked me to my core. I wasn't sure I could relinquish myself to this kind of hope and longing and potential heartbreak again.

But destiny doesn't have much interest in our uncertainty, does it? It kind of does its thing, with or without our permission. And thank God. Three months later, we were matched with another birth mother. She was six months along when we met face-to-face for the first time— we talked about her dreams and ours and we decided to go down this road together. While we had specified with the failed adoption that we wanted a baby girl, this time we decided it wasn't that important. We'd wait and see when the baby was born. A month before her due date, however, the birth mother *did* find out the baby's gender and took great pride in telling us our daughter was on the way.

On March 8, 2009, which also happens to be our wedding anniversary, Lennox Esmée Wilson was born. She was perfection. We gazed into her eyes in amazement that she was ours. I didn't want to look away. Or even blink. Or miss one fraction of a second with my daughter.

I remember asking Dave that day what he would say to the first birth mother, the one who changed her mind. He said, "I'd say 'thank you.'"

I believe there is a special place in heaven for birth mothers who choose adoption for their babies. It is a courageous and selfless act that expands the amount of love in the world. It has certainly expanded the amount of love in *our* world. And we are eternally grateful for our girl.

ASK A SILLY QUESTION

———

Because Lennox doesn't look like us, some people have trouble understanding that she really is *our daughter*. People stop me in the grocery store and say, "She's so beautiful. Do you know her real father?" "Yes," I say, "I know him *very* well. I've been sleeping with him for years." That response—which I always give with a good-natured smile—is not meant to shame or scold people whose intentions I know are good. It's intended to get a laugh and make people think about their assumptions, and perhaps reconsider their definition of what makes a father "real."

They also ask if I know her real mother. To which I usually laugh and say, "Quite well. I'm Kortney, her real mother. Nice to meet you!" I'm lighthearted about it and not condescending, because I know they are just curious. I usually follow up with: "I'm kidding; I know you meant 'birth mother.'"

"She's so lucky to have you" is the one we get most often. "Not sure about that," I say, "but we certainly feel lucky to have *her*." Again, I know these people are well meaning. They are trying to offer support or a stamp of approval, without considering whether I want or need their approval. Or considering what their opinion might mean to Lennox, whose brothers are never told by strangers how lucky *they* are to have us as parents. I happen to think we're good parents, but the fact that we adopted a child doesn't make it so.

DAVE: *My personal favorite is "Is she yours?"*

KORTNEY: *To which I always reply, "Yes, why? Don't you think she looks like me?"*

I said that once to a 10-year-old girl at the pool, and she paused and looked at me and Lennox for a good 10 seconds, then said, "She has your chin." To this day, Lennox and I joke that we have the same chin.

DAVE: *You kind of do have the same chin.*

KORTNEY: *Like mother, like daughter, right?*

I try to be playful with my responses in an effort to educate people, gently. My hope is that when they ask a silly question or make an insensitive remark, my silly answer will get them to pause and *think* about how their words might be received.

LIGHT IT RIGHT

———

There are always candles burning in our home. The warm light and subtle fragrance have an instant calming effect on me, so I try to make sure there's a lit candle wherever I am in the house. But what many people, including Dave, don't realize is that there's a right way and a wrong way to light a candle—and when you light a candle the wrong way, you shorten its lifespan and decrease its beauty.

DAVE: *So I'm basically a candle murderer.*

KORTNEY: *Pretty much.*

DAVE: *Teach us your ways, then, high priestess of Candletopia.*

KORTNEY: *I thought you'd never ask.*

The Right Way to Light a Candle

1. **Trim the wick.** Before you light a candle, trim the tip of the wick with scissors or nail clippers. A freshly trimmed wick will produce a brighter, more even flame and no smoke. (If your candle happens to be in a glass container, that means the sides of the glass won't fog up or blacken over time.)

2. **Let it burn!** You can't light a candle and blow it out 10 minutes later. You have to let the wax melt all the way across the candle's surface, which can take about an hour. This way, when it cools, you're left with a flat surface like the one you started with. If you light the candle and blow it out too soon, only the center wax will melt, and the wick

will start to sink down into a sad little tunnel, where eventually it will be impossible to light.

DAVE: *And all the nearby angels will weep.*

KORTNEY: *Or at the very least, your wife will weep, knowing she didn't get full use of her $18 candle.*

DAVE: *Speaking of "getting full use of your candle," don't forget the spaghetti lighter.*

3. **Yes! The spaghetti lighter method.** Instead of lighting your candle with a match, light a stick of raw spaghetti. It's long, so you won't burn your fingers, and it burns forever, so you can actually light multiple candles before the spaghetti goes out. This is especially handy for lighting nearly spent candles in deep glass containers.

KORTNEY: *You've redeemed yourself with that tip, Dave. Thank you.*

DAVE: *Never underestimate your old flame.*

DAVE WILSON MASTER CLASS
KEEP THESE HANDYPERSON FAVORITES HANDY

—

I'm not a "gear guy." I don't insist on top-of-the-line tools or fancy military-grade flashlights. My favorite multi-bit screwdriver cost about $15, and it works like a charm. Actually, it works like 11 charms, which is quite a bargain. I'm all about finding the simplest, most effective tool to get the job done. And if that tool costs me $1.09 at the Dollar Holler, which the majority of the tools in our handyperson survival kit did, even better.

What's in Our Handyperson Survival Kit?

- **Let's start with the word "handyperson."** When you're married to Kortney, your odds of survival increase greatly with the use of gender-neutral terms. Especially when she does more than 50 percent of the household handy things.

- **The basics.** Hammer, multi-bit screwdriver, razor blade, adhesive bandages (because of the razor blade), tape measure, flashlight, matches, candles, raw spaghetti.

- **Yes, I said "raw spaghetti."** I said it before, and I'll say it again. It's the ultimate multi-tool. Boil it and it's delicious. Light a stick on fire and it will burn long enough to light every candle in the house when the power goes out. Light the candles, then boil the rest of the spaghetti, and you can have a romantic candlelit dinner. Bam. Toolbox 101.

- **Vaseline.** After that candlelit dinner . . . *I'm joking. You people are disgusting!* Vaseline happens to have many practical household uses. Use it to unstick a zipper, lubricate a light bulb's metal threads before you screw it in, so it won't rust, or—my personal favorite—use it as a substitute for painter's tape. If you're refinishing a piece of furniture and you're too lazy to remove the hardware (which I am), apply a little Vaseline to the hardware, then wipe it off when the paint dries. Do not attempt to smear Vaseline all over the baseboards when painting your living room, however. Painter's tape is a safer bet there. Don't ask me how I know.

- **A paintbrush for dusting baseboards.** Kortney schooled me on this one. Instead of using a wet wipe to clean the baseboards (which will leave a wife-angering smear in its wake), use a clean, dry paintbrush and simply sweep the dirt away.

- **Wood-colored pens.** These are special wood-colored paint pens that cover nicks and scuffs in your hardwood floors. Kortney likes to include these in her welcome baskets for new neighbors. I like to include them in my pocket every time I go to move the furniture and forget to use the next item on this list.

- **Self-stick felt pads.** These are the little soft circles you stick to the feet of your furniture to keep them from scuffing up the floors. I keep them in my toolbox at all times, which is why I'm constantly scratching up the floors every time I move the furniture. The whole point of these is that they go *on the furniture*, NOT in your toolbox.

- **A stud finder.** Sadly, this is one tool where you get what you pay for. The more studs you want to find, the more you have to spend on a stud finder. When they work, they're worth their weight in gold. When they don't, they're worth their weight in all of the unnecessary holes you hammered into your drywall while your wife eyeballed you in disgust, thinking, *Damn it; I thought I'd found myself a stud.*

GET THE KIDS
THEIR OWN HOUSE

Neither Dave nor I had a tree house growing up. It wasn't something we ever talked about, but when our kids were little and we bought the house we live in now, it became very apparent that Dave had been living with an enormous tree-house-shaped hole in his heart. And he was going to fill that hole with a tree house—whether our kids were asking for one or not. (They weren't.)

Our house had a big deck in back with an old hackberry growing out of it. Dave decided he was going to take out the deck and replace it with the tree house to end all tree houses.

DAVE: *Also known as "the tree house to end all savings accounts."*

He got to work, building the house up and around the hackberry tree. My dad drove to Nashville to help. Dave had no blueprints—just a head filled with tree house dreams. He ended up spending a fortune, but I didn't say a word. This was his baby. My only suggestion was that he give the house a clear Plexiglas roof, so it would have plenty of light during the day—and the kids could see the stars through the roof at night.

DAVE: *That was a good call. And one of the few things we did right when building that thing.*

The tree house itself was beautiful. But little did we know hackberries are not sturdy trees. This one was particularly old and tall and prone to splitting. An arborist warned us that one hurricane or tornado would take it down, and our house with it. The hackberry had to go. If you've ever had to remove a tree, you know what an expensive endeavor it can be. If you've ever had to remove a tree *with a tree house around it*, your wallet is at least a thousand dollars lighter than it used to be. And that's not counting the cost to rebuild the tree house floor.

There are actual houses in our neighborhood that cost less than this tree house. But I'd still have Dave do it all over again. Only after the kids saw what their dad (and mine) had built did they realize the magic of having a place to truly call their own. We let them paint and

decorate the interior any way they wanted. I believe one side says "Girls Rule, Boys Drool" and the other says "No Girls Allowed." Somehow this makes everyone feel welcome.

The kids have sleepovers in the tree house to this day. In fact, they use it more now than they did when they were younger. When we throw parties, the downstairs of the treehouse now serves as a buffet, and the kids and their friends play bartender, serving up snacks and drinks. Later the younger ones can retreat to the kids-only zone upstairs, while the older boys shoot hoops on the back wall.

If you have the space and inclination to build a tree house, I highly recommend it.

Tips for Building a Treehouse

Know thy trees. Building around the hackberry was a rookie mistake that cost us. If you must put the "tree" in "tree house" (and you really don't have to, since the structure doesn't actually touch the tree), do your research on what kind of tree you're working with.

Let the light in. Not only will it make the space light and airy and more pleasant to spend time in, but it will keep the bugs away. Darkness and wood attract spiders and insects, which repel children and defeat the whole purpose of getting them their own place.

Hire an expert. A prefabricated tree house would have saved us a ton of money, but Dave was determined to make this a custom masterpiece. A little expert help on the front end—and a conversation with an arborist—would have saved us considerable time and expense.

Build for the future. To Dave's credit, he built a tree house that would grow with the kids. The space was big enough and flexible enough to be reconfigured over time. We've since added a basketball net and the downstairs "bar" area, which makes a great party zone.

Keep out. Let the kids have the place to themselves. Let them paint and decorate and put up posters and signs. Knowing they have one place where mom's not going to meddle with the design (or tell them to clean up) is empowering for them—and it's high enough off the ground that you don't have to see it.

DAVE WILSON MASTER CLASS
TAKE THE CAMPING TEST

I have one of those friends who thinks he's madly in love after just the second date.

I mean, every single time.

Finally, I explained to him that, before he decides he's in love with a woman, she must first pass the camping test. The camping test is when you invite her to go camping and "forget" to bring four major camping supplies. I'm talking lighters, sleeping bags, flashlights, food. The biggies. If she loses her mind and hates it, run. If she laughs or, better yet, has brought the supplies herself—knowing you would probably forget them—MARRY HER.

KORTNEY: *It's a good thing we were already married with two kids when you tested this out on me.*

DAVE: *I like to test-drive my own advice on a closed course. For safety purposes.*

KORTNEY: *So I was like your camping crash test dummy?*

DAVE: *I'm pretty sure I was the dummy, and you were the one who remembered the first aid kit. One of the many reasons I married you.*

KORTNEY: *I also remembered the tent and the rain cover, which is the only reason we stayed dry.*

DAVE: *Dry, and married.*

SHE'S A BRICK HOUSE . . . PAINT HER

I love brick. Interior brick, exterior brick, pristine or painted, I love it all.

One of my favorite things about demo day is unexpectedly uncovering brick that a previous owner has seen fit to cover up or tile over. It's like finding buried treasure, and I will go to great lengths to salvage it. Lucky for me, these happy surprises are quite common, especially in older houses.

Case in point: before we bought our Victorian home years ago, we were chatting with the man who owned it. I mentioned that the first thing I'd do would be to uncover all of the brick on the eight original fireplaces.

He told me there wasn't any.

DAVE: *Which was his first mistake.*

So I ran to the car and grabbed a hammer.

DAVE: *Which was kind of a turn-on, not gonna lie.*

"Mind if I have a look?" I asked (seeing as he was about to take it back down to the studs).

He said, "Go right ahead. I'm telling you, there's nothing but tile under there."

DAVE: *Mistake number two.*

I jabbed a hole through the wall, and sure enough, he was right. Tile. From the '80s. Which is a sure sign that behind it is *brick* . . . from the 1800s.

DAVE: *But you didn't tell him that. Instead, you just told him he was right and we should draw up an offer.*

KORTNEY: *It was a calculated business move. Plus, there was no convincing him. He was sure that all eight fireplaces were built out of tile.*

So we bought the house and uncovered the fireplace brick, all of which was basically intact. Two were pristine. Four needed sealant, and the other two needed quite a bit of patchwork.

Those were the two we ended up having to paint to give them a cohesive feel.

DAVE: *That painting was the beginning of my baldness.*

KORTNEY: *You were bald long before we started painting brick.*

And if we hadn't painted them, the patches would have distracted from the brick itself.

DAVE: *I still didn't love the idea.*

KORTNEY: *You acted like I was trying to pierce our daughter's belly button. With salad tongs.*

Granted, it's not always my first choice to paint brick (I did leave the other fireplaces fully exposed), but sometimes it's the right thing to do. And this was definitely one of those times.
 I can't say this enough. Design is a balancing act. The rules are there to guide you, but don't be so beholden to them that you become paralyzed with indecision or—worse—driven to bad decisions. It's that kind of rigid rule following that leads to brick being covered up in the first place! (Well, we can't paint it to match the room, so let's cover it up.)

DAVE: *You say "rigid rule following." I say "bad taste."*

KORTNEY: *Tomato, tomahto.*

DAVE: *(But really just tomahto.)*

Now, when it comes to a home's exterior, I love a painted brick house. In fact, I'd consider building a house out of brick *just so I can paint it.*

DAVE: *I'm pretty sure 50 percent of our readers are about to drop dead.*

KORTNEY: *Including your father.*

DAVE: *DON'T GO TOWARD THE LIGHT, DAD. NO ONE IS PAINTING ANY BRICK, DAD.*

Speaking of not painting brick, last season we painted *all but one* of the brick houses, because Dave begged me to leave the last one natural. I spent hours selecting accent colors that would make the brick look appealing to buyers. Turns out the buyers loved the house *in spite* of the brick, because two weeks after we closed, I drove by and they'd painted the entire house white.

DAVE: *[Holds up a "You Were Right" sign]*

People are coming around on this one, I'm telling you. Once you give yourself permission to paint brick, you open up a world of possibilities. Bright whites and dark, moody hues—you can do anything.

DAVE: *Ooh, speaking of . . . tell them about that water thing you do.*

KORTNEY: *You mean whitewashing?*

Whitewashing is a very happy medium. It's essentially applying watered-down paint and letting the color of the brick seep through. The more color you want to see, the more water you add to the paint. The process is easy, and it gives you a gorgeous distressed look when you're through.

DAVE: *Speaking of distress, may I suggest that whatever color you decide to paint, you rent a sprayer. Painting brick by hand is like brushing your hair with a spoon. Not productive.*

How to Paint Brick (Somewhat) Painlessly

1. **Definitely rent a sprayer,** especially if you're painting exteriors or large areas of brick. Dave Wilson painting brick by hand is *not* the distressed look anyone is going for.

2. **Start with a clean slate.** Wash or power-wash brick with warm water and allow it to dry for at least 24 hours. Longer if you live in a warm or humid climate.

3. **Prime it.** One coat should do the trick. Two if the brick is more porous or textured.

4. **Paint and enjoy.** And don't worry for one second about the naysayers. They literally don't know what they're missing.

TAKE PICTURES
OF THEIR PICTURES

———

A friend of mine recently told me she has kept *every piece of art* her child has ever made. Every piece! Let's pause for a moment and do the math on this, shall we? Her daughter is eight years old and has attended some form of school six out of those eight years. If you multiply six years by 180 instructional days and add 70,000 pieces of elbow macaroni, nine bushels of yarn, 16 containers of rubber cement, 2,500 sheets of construction paper, and divide the whole thing by the square root of papier-mâché, what do you get?

DAVE: *A divorce?*

KORTNEY: *EXACTLY. Who has the physical space—or the headspace—for all of that art?*

That's why I tell mamas to be more like MoMA, and *curate the heck out of their kids'*

art collections. If something adorable comes home (or something *not* adorable that the kid is really proud of), it goes on the art board for one month. Tops. After that, I recycle it, toss it, or mail it to the grandparents so *they* can toss it. I'm KIDDING.

DAVE: *She's not kidding.*

KORTNEY: *Not even a little.*

Call me unsentimental, but if you bring home a brown-paper lunch sack with two sequins glued to its "face" and tell me it's a dog puppet, it's probably not going in the permanent collection.

That said, I'm not a heartless person. And I know that one day I'll want to look back on these years of artistic abundance, which is why I've learned to save the kids' art the Kortney Wilson way.

Take Pictures of Their Pictures

1. Before I (ahem) *relocate* one of the kid's masterpieces, I snap a picture of it. Or, if the artist is available, I'll snap a picture of him or her holding the art.

2. I upload the photo to an online storage folder.

3. At the end of every school year, I import the folder into one of those online photo services and make myself a book of their greatest hits.

4. I order a hardbound copy to keep on the coffee table.

If you *want* to keep your kids' original artwork (and you live in an airplane hangar), by all means do so. But if you're only doing it out of guilt—or fear of forgetting—my little system serves the same purpose and takes up way less space. Also? While I did say I'm not overly sentimental, I have been known to shed quite a few tears turning those precious pages.

KNOW YOUR HONEY, WHEN IT COMES TO MONEY

———

Dave is an eternal optimist, whereas I walk Realism Boulevard all day long.

DAVE: *With a pied-à-terre on Grumpy Pessimist Lane.*

I like to hope for the best and prepare for the worst, and that applies to everything, including money. Though we come from different financial backgrounds, when Dave and I met, we were both broke and determined to make it on our own, without borrowing money from anyone. When we moved in together, we agreed to live by the same financial rules.

DAVE: *Kortney's rules.*

We would not spend more than we made. And we would not go into debt. We lived in a tiny little apartment, in a building that resembled a portable classroom. It was cheap and poorly insulated, and come November, our heating bill jumped from $50 to $290. When I got the bill, I called Dave in a panic—but not before turning off the heat. All that winter we slept in sweaters and coats and as many socks as we could layer on our feet, until the advance payment came in from my record label.

DAVE: *We knew the money was coming.*

KORTNEY: We thought *the money was coming.*

But until that money was in the bank, we wore layers.

DAVE: *Lots and lots of layers.*

Once we had a bit of a financial cushion, I still wanted to be careful.

DAVE: *And I wanted to eat meals that didn't come from a can.*

We had to learn to compromise.

DAVE: *I had to learn to enter chewing-gum expenditures into a spreadsheet.*

I wanted to see our true cost of living.

DAVE: *Big Red. $0.79.*

I wasn't begrudging Dave that pack of gum—or even dictating what we could and could not buy—I just needed a clear picture of what we were spending. And Dave, who has a much higher tolerance for risk than I do—

DAVE: *And a higher tolerance for fun . . .*

—was able to take more risks *and have more fun* as long as I could *see* that we could afford it. That was our compromise.

Over time, we ditched the spreadsheet in favor of more sophisticated money-management tools.

DAVE: *In favor of staying married.*

And Dave continues to remind me that it's okay to enjoy the fruits of our labor, to take vacations, and treat ourselves—as long as we're living within our means.

DAVE: *Work hard, play hard.*

KORTNEY: *And save hard.*

DAVE: *But not too hard. It's all about balance.*

KORTNEY: *While keeping an eye on the account balance.*

DAVE: *And occasionally closing your eyes and leaping into the unknown . . .*

KORTNEY: *As long as there's a financial cushion to break your fall.*

TACKLE THE TINY TASKS FIRST

———

I used to listen to a radio talk show where people would call in to ask the host for financial advice, mainly related to digging their way out of debt. Without fail, the callers would talk about how long they'd been paying down their largest debt and how, even though they'd been diligently chipping away at it, it barely seemed to make a dent. At this point in the program, the host would stop the caller and call them out for being not just broke—but *stupid*. He was of the opinion that paying off the smallest debts first would be faster and easier, leading to a greater sense of accomplishment that would fuel a person's desire to stay the course. (It also freed up funds to throw at the bigger debt when the small ones were paid off.) His delivery was a little salty, but the advice was solid. And I immediately recognized it as being applicable to other areas of my life as well.

Think of your to-do list. What will make you feel more accomplished? Slaving away at the toughest task—or knocking out the fast and easy items first, so you can check some boxes and feel like the rock star you are? For me, it's far and away the latter. I love checking things off my to-do list. Sometimes I'll even accomplish something that wasn't on my to-do list, and I'll write it down just so I can check it off, because it's JUST. SO. SATISFYING.

DAVE: *You add things to your to-do list after they're done, just so you can say you did them?*

KORTNEY: *You say that as if it's crazy.*

DAVE: *Because it is crazy.*

KORTNEY: *Burping the alphabet is crazy. Adding something to your to-do list so you can luxuriate in the profound pleasure of checking it off is 100 percent logical. And I defy you to find a single woman who disagrees with me.*

Tackle the tiniest tasks first. Cleaning out the medicine cabinet. Check! Decluttering the hall closet. Check! Knock out one extra thing every weekend until it becomes habitual. Those check marks are addictive and intoxicating, and the more you rack up, the more motivated you'll be to master bigger and better tasks, like that one that was weighing you down and keeping you from doing *anything at all.*

DITCH YOUR DESIGN ANXIETY

———

I have always been energized and inspired by change. But most people I meet say that change makes them uneasy or, in some cases, completely unhinged. They *want* to make a change—but they find the process paralyzing. I remind them that interior design is not rocket science or brain surgery, and that even if that couch they just bought won't fit through the front door, and their spouse's eyes are shooting daggers, no lives are *actually* on the line.

DAVE: *I have scars from your eyeball daggers, actually.*

KORTNEY: *Those are emotional scars. They'll heal.*

DAVE: *You're such a nurturer.*

Sometimes we need tough love. And for the change-haters, I've got a news flash: change is not the problem. Fear is. And fear may be standing between you and your dream house. Or your dream living room. Or your dream couch.

DAVE: *Or a recliner that doesn't smell like pet urine.*

KORTNEY: *That's disgusting, but yes, you have the basic idea. Even small decisions can be paralyzing for some people.*

So, the first thing you have to do is identify the source (or sources) of your anxiety. Are you overwhelmed by the sheer size and scope of the task at hand? Maybe money's the issue, and you're afraid of making a costly mistake. Or perhaps you just don't trust your own eyes —or your own taste.

Whatever your fear, there's a fix.

My Favorite Ways to Oust Anxiety

Break it down into bite-size tasks. If there's anything I've learned from flipping houses, it's this: *there's no such thing as a big job.* Every big job is really just a collection of smaller tasks when you break it down. And that's exactly what you have to do: break it down. Instead of

assigning yourself an entire living room make-over, why not start with one wall?

DAVE: *What if one wall overwhelms me?*

KORTNEY: *Break it down again.*

Flip through a magazine and find some colors you like, then walk away. Tomorrow, maybe you'll head to the paint store and pick up some samples. Over the weekend, you can paint a few test stripes and live with them for a day or two. Give yourself permission to take it step by step, and pat yourself on the back for even the smallest accomplishment.

A quick word of caution. This "break it down" advice is a great cure for the overwhelmed, but if you're one of those people who starts 50 projects and never finishes any of them, your problem isn't fear—it's follow-through. For you, I recommend *scheduling* the steps (one a day, one a week, whatever) until you get the job done. No starting anything new until the first project's complete.

DAVE: *Would you like me to hold your soapbox, or are you still using it?*

KORTNEY: *I'm done.*

Afraid of making a costly mistake? Go neutral.
White. Beige. Gray. Taupe. God was not lacking in imagination when she created 50 shades of ecru. The variety of can't-go-wrong whites is the gift that keeps on giving. When you're shelling out for big-ticket items (think couches, area rugs, tile, countertops), let neutrals be your safety net. Don't get me wrong; I'm all for rocking the color boat, but there are less expensive ways to do it. If you're worried about budget, go wild with accents (pillows, candles, prints, even walls) and play it safe with the rest.

Don't trust your own taste? Call a friend.
I have a friend who is gorgeous and witty and bright and completely incapable of making design decisions on her own. She will stare at a wall full of grays for three weeks, paralyzed by the choices (when, in fact, any one of them would work just fine). If she enjoyed wallowing in indecision, that would be one thing, but it seriously stresses her out to be stuck in design limbo. So, now she calls me. I'll run down the street, spend two minutes looking at her swatch wall, and say, "That one!" And our rule is, she has to do whatever I say and move on. If analysis paralysis is what's plaguing you, outsource the decision-making to someone whose taste you trust, and agree that, in exchange for their advice, you will follow it. This takes the pressure off in two ways. One, you're no longer in charge. And two, you're no longer responsible if it all goes horribly wrong. Ha! I'm kidding. The fact is, it's pretty hard for someone with a good eye to make a colossally bad decision. So take the pressure off yourself and hand it to someone who loves telling you what to do.

LOVE YOUR SELFIE

———

I love selfies. Always have. Probably always will. And at this more public moment in my life, the selfie is practically a job requirement. But even if it weren't, I'd be an unapologetic fan of the art form (and *yes*, it is an art form).

If you still think selfies are for nitwits and narcissists, maybe I can help *reframe* them for you.

I am a boss lady. A woman in charge.

I am in charge of my career. I am in charge of a team of people. I am in charge of my home. I (with Dave's partnership, of course) am in charge of my kids and raising them to be kind, upstanding humans.

I am in charge of their education.

I am in charge of my life.

So I can *damn well* be in charge of taking my own picture. See how that works?

Maybe you've noticed that when someone else takes your picture, it doesn't always look like you. Or at least it doesn't look like the "you" you see when you look in the mirror. That's not so with selfies, where you can control the angles, the light, and the look on your face. Not to mention the almighty DELETE button when you don't quite nail the look you were going for.

Now, not all selfies are created equal. So if you're new to the art, my secrets—born of *lots* of trial and error—are here for the taking:

My Selfie Secrets

- **Look into the light.** Unless you're having a near-death experience, this is the time to go toward the light. Whether it's a lamp, a bonfire, or that big golden ball in the sky, that's the direction you should be looking in. If the light is behind you, your face will be in shadow, and that is not a good look for the modern-day girl (or guy) boss.

- **Lens high, chin low.** You want to be looking slightly up at the camera, but only with your *eyes*, not your whole face. And don't take it to the extreme. If you hoist the camera over your head like a flag, you'll look like a walking forehead. Go easy on yourself.

- **Be yourself.** There are photographers out there who will tell you that a fake smile looks more real than a real smile when it comes to being on camera. They actually *teach* this. And it's complete and utter bull honky. These poor women, whose real-life smiles are beautiful and relaxed and genuine, get in front of a camera and grin like they're getting a mammogram. It's not a good look. And it completely defeats the empowering purpose of the selfie! Smile your real smile. Or stick out your tongue if that's more your style. But don't let anyone tell you to manufacture a smile that's not your own so you can look more beautiful. Not. Cool.

- **Don't overedit.** The abundance of photo-editing apps is overwhelmingly awesome. You can smooth out your skin, apply make-up in postproduction, increase the size of your eyes, or even change their color. My suggestion? Don't. It's one thing to have fun with filters (the Nashville filter on Insta-gram happens to be the *bomb*), but when it comes to your face, empower yourself to keep it real. (That said, I am not the boss of you, and if you want to digitally ditch your pores, that's entirely your business.)

- **Practice makes perfect.** There's a reason selfie-haters hate my selfies. *I take a lot of them.* Learn what lighting and angles work for you, and you'll become an expert in no

time. You'll also connect with a lot of people who *like* seeing the real you and double-tap their approval to tell you so.

- **Have a sense of humor.** We can analyze the psychology behind the rise of "selfie culture" and its social consequences all day long, *or* we could use that time for more soul-satisfying pursuits, like posing for "twinsie" pics with our pets. I don't take any of this selfie stuff all that seriously, and neither should you. It's just a fun way to be yourself and see yourself—and let the world see you too.

- **Don't apologize.** You are the boss of you. And you are the boss of your selfies. If you find that it's a fun way to connect with people over social media (or just a super convenient way to check your makeup), don't let the selfie police stand in your way. Selfies are about honoring life's happy moments—and capturing them as *you* want to remember them.

CHIN TOO LOW

CHIN TOO HIGH

OO DARK

JUST RIGHT

PERFORM A $100 MAKEOVER MIRACLE

As much as I love a gut-to-the-studs renovation, sometimes a mini makeover is all I need to maximize my enjoyment of a space. While not everyone embraces change as wholeheartedly as I do, most people will at least admit that a room refresh feels good for the soul. It doesn't have to be dramatic, expensive, or time-consuming either. In fact, I do this in my own home a couple of times a year.

Give One Room a Mini Makeover

1. **Declutter.** Old magazines on the coffee table? Recycle them. Nine thousand packs of soy sauce in the utensil drawer? Sayonara. Be ruthless with the room you choose. Fill a bag to the brim and feel the stress leaving your body.

2. **Paint.** Have I mentioned the transformative power of paint? Even a fresh coat of white on the baseboards can work wonders—but if you're headed to the paint store anyway, why not try a new shade on for size? Choose a color that coordinates with your existing furniture, though, or you'll have more than a mini makeover on your hands.

3. **Stage/rearrange.** Not every space can accommodate a complete reconfiguration of existing furniture. In some rooms there will be only one logical place to put a sofa. That doesn't mean you have to skip this step altogether. Cast a critical eye over your current setup and consider what would happen if you rotated the whole thing a quarter turn clockwise. This forces you to envision every element in a different location. Not all of it will work, of course, but you're almost guaranteed to get ideas. Moving that one lamp or swapping those side tables could breathe new life into the room and lets you experience it in a whole new way.

4. **Accessorize.** Never underestimate the power of a blanket, some throw pillows, and a pretty potted plant. I call this combo the $100 makeover miracle, because even without steps 2 and 3 (sorry, friends, but the decluttering step is nonnegotiable), these

three items—in a color you've never considered before—can make a room feel like new.

5. **Light.** Could your space stand to be brighter? Up the wattage or add a new accent lamp. Or maybe a moodier vibe would make the room more appealing, in which case you might dim the ambient lights and bring the accent lamps in from the far corners, closer to the furniture configuration.

Every space is unique, so what works in one room won't work in others. Nevertheless, the five-step approach makes you stop and address all of the areas that could potentially use an update. Even if you only make a minor change in all five areas, the total result can have a major impact on how much you enjoy your space.

DAVE: *If I may, I'd like to interject one additional piece of advice here.*

KORTNEY: *By all means.*

DAVE: *Do not, under any circumstances, attempt a mini makeover when your wife is out of town. Remember when I tried to surprise you by rearranging all of the furniture in our bedroom?*

KORTNEY: *Oh, you definitely surprised me.*

DAVE: *Yeah, just not in the way I'd hoped.*

KORTNEY: *I felt so bad. You were so proud of yourself and it was just—all wrong. After I'd spent months getting that room just right. I had to pretend I liked it.*

DAVE: *So, when you walked in and said, "What the f*ck did you do, Dave?" that was you pretending you liked it?*

KORTNEY: *Well, I wasn't pretending very hard.*

DAVE: *You didn't even take your coat off before you started putting everything back the way it was.*

KORTNEY: *So maybe we need a different set of steps for you?*

DAVE: *Yes.*

HERE YOU GO, DAVE:

1. **Declutter.** This step is very difficult (but not impossible) to screw up.

2. **Grab yourself a beer.** All rooms look better when you're holding a beer.

3. **There are no more steps.** At this point, you will only make things worse, so you should probably just go watch hockey.

BUILD SHELVES
OUT OF REACH

———

When Dave and I were renovating our own house years ago, I found myself in an almost heated conversation with the carpenter who we'd hired to build some open shelving in our kitchen. I was in the car on the way to the airport, trying to sketch out my design on a napkin so I could better explain it to him. Sketching is *not* my strong suit, so I quickly gave up and said, "Look, just take the shelves all the way up to the ceiling. I don't care about the shelf sizes—they don't have to be standard, and they don't have to be uniform—but the whole unit MUST go floor to ceiling."

He then had the nerve to ask why a "tiny gal like me" would do with 14-foot shelves.

DAVE: *Did you tell him what a tiny gal like you would do with a wiseass carpenter?*

KORTNEY: *I was tempted. But I was also going out of town, and I really didn't want him screwing up the shelves to spite me while I was away.*

DAVE: *Smart move. Revenge is not a dish best served by a guy with a circular saw.*

Thankfully, Prince Charming followed my instructions, and the result was (surprise, surprise) *dramatic and gorgeous*. At that point, the open shelving was the focal point of our kitchen and a place for me to display some things that were meaningful to me.

DAVE: *And a place to display my mom's broken heirloom so she couldn't get up close and see where you'd glued it back together.*

KORTNEY: *Exactly. That's not something you can do with six-foot shelves, my friend.*

Even if you have nothing to hide, I *highly* recommend building shelves all the way up to the ceiling. Stopping several feet short leaves you with nothing but unusable wall space and a nice ledge for collecting dust (or displaying fake potted plants that collect dust). Better to take those "dust collectors" all the way up to the ceiling so they can make themselves useful. The height of the shelves will accentuate the height of the room and make rooms with average-height ceilings feel bigger than they are. Yes, more materials means greater cost, but the extra height will not only add to your enjoyment of the space, it will likely add value to your home in the long run.

Where Else Should You Go Higher?

Kitchen cabinets. When I'm renovating or building a kitchen from scratch, kitchen cabinets that go all the way up to the ceiling are an absolute must for me, design-wise. They're also so much more practical than their standard squatty cousins. But let's say you want to refurbish a kitchen in which the standard-height cabinets are in perfectly good condition. In this case, you can fake it. Hire a carpenter to build open boxes (square shelves) on top of the cabinets, then paint the wall, shelves, and cabinets the same color for a cohesive look. Top it all off with some crown molding and *voilà*: "custom" cabinets.

Stove hood vent. Consider building a box around the stainless steel vent that goes all the way to the ceiling and topping it off with crown molding. Or you can buy a wall hood extension kit, so the unit itself appears to vent to the ceiling. Dave used to fight me on this one, saying it was an unnecessary expense for something most people don't notice. But people *do* notice. They may not be able to pinpoint *why* the kitchen feels so put together, but then they'll comment on how much they love our stove—when they have the exact same one. Details make a difference.

Tile backsplash. It's as simple as this: I would rather you select a much less expensive tile (white subway tile is as cheap as it gets) and take it *all* the way to the ceiling than spend $20 per square foot on tile and only buy enough to go 6 or 7 inches (15 or 18 centimeters) up from the counter. No matter how beautiful the tile, if you don't take it all the way up, it's going to feel unfinished.

STORE EVERYTHING IN PLAIN SIGHT

For me, closed storage is a necessary evil. There are some things in life that beg to be kept out of sight (think tampons and toiletries, garbage bags and bulk items), but for every one of those, there are five or six others that could be beautifully displayed in broad daylight, if people would simply open their minds (and their shelves).

My closet is a great example of this. Many closet companies want to come in and build grand armoires with doors and drawers, but I want to see everything. The same goes for nightstands, pantries, and general shelving. Show me what we've got!

We have one closet in our house where I store gifts and gift wrap for future occasions, and it's all closed off, with various doors and drawers for scissors and tape and ribbons and bows. While it sounds like Mrs. Claus's dream come true, I kind of hate it. Turns out you can't just leave a couple of rolls of wrapping paper alone together behind closed doors and assume the best. When you return, there will no doubt be three additional rolls and a bag of stick-on bows that you don't remember buying. I'll buy a funny little book for a girlfriend's upcoming birthday, and when I go to pull it out of the bag and wrap it one month later, it's living with a scarf, a gardening journal, and a lollipop that is also a flashlight. Unacceptable.

DAVE: *Are you saying that the lollipop flashlight started subletting our closet without your consent?*

KORTNEY: *I'm saying there's no lease agreement with my signature on it.*

DAVE: *Do you think it's possible that you bought the lollipop flashlight as a gift for one of the kid's friends and forgot about it?*

KORTNEY: *I think anything is possible. ANYTHING AT ALL. As soon as you close a closet door, you have relinquished control. There's no telling what's happening in there.*

I remember seeing the Nancy Meyers movie *It's Complicated*, with Meryl Streep, and

drooling over her character's kitchen—which was anything but complicated, despite the fact that everything in it was stored in plain sight. Pots and utensils within arm's reach. Dishes of different shapes and sizes stacked on open shelves. Appliances out and ready to use. Bowls brimming with fruit on the counters. It was a set, of course, but it sure didn't feel like one. That kitchen felt real, like years of memories that had been made there. It felt lived in, without being the least bit cluttered.

That's how I want my life to feel. Our kitchen, our bathrooms, our closets. I do my best to store everything *as if* it's all open storage—like someone might come to open my pantry at any moment.

Open Storage Tips

Fold and stack. For example, I love the look of extra blankets in coordinating colors, folded and stacked on an open shelf. Or, instead of hiding my cutting boards in a drawer, I'll stack several horizontally and set a small easel on top to display my handmade favorite. I bought it because it was beautiful and practical, so it's practical to store it where I can see it.

Check your levels. With open shelving, the goal is to create continuity but not *uniformity*. After all, this is your home, not a Pottery Barn. So pay attention to the flow of items, varying widths and heights and mixing up vertically oriented pieces with others displayed horizontally (like the cutting boards above).

Group and balance colors. If you find yourself with a shelf full of color, group like colors together and use neutral elements to create space in between.

Or stick with neutrals and add a pop of color throughout. Warm grays, whites, and ivories, mixed with wood grains by way of baskets and rustic frames, give your space a cohesive look, while pops of a bold accent color bring it to life. Imagine, for example, a shelf of bone ceramic dishes in various heights and stacks, with a red vase in one spot and a pretty collection of coffee cups with red writing in another. Perhaps on the table there's a red runner or red napkins as well. Because neutrals recede and colors pop, this technique will make the space feel open, as opposed to overwhelming.

Store healthy foods where you can see them. It's so easy to reach for ready-made foods. But when I store beans and grains in mason jars of various sizes out in the open, where I can see them, not only do I know what I have in stock, I'm way more inclined to use what I've got.

Just add art. Art is a great way to personalize open shelving and make everything on it feel deliberate. A cool sculpture or painting propped up among more functional items says everything displayed here is "here by choice" not "here by chance."

While the popularity of open shelving ebbs and flows (and seems to be trending downward at the moment), thoughtful storage solutions built into every room are always going to be in style. A chest built into a window seat, for example, where you can store blankets and pillows that swap out with the seasons, is what I call smart storage.

DAVE: *At least it seems smart until you reach in there for the winter blankets and pull out a bag of dog food and a half-eaten donut.*

KORTNEY: *Hence my preference for open storage.*

The bottom line is this: When it comes to storage, out of sight means out of mind. And out of mind means out of control.

DAVE: *And being out of control means Kortney loses her mind, which means the more open shelving, the better. At least for us. But you can do what you want because it's your life. The end.*

SEND SNAIL MAIL

———

I loved getting mail when I was a kid, didn't you? It hardly mattered what it was—I just liked that it was addressed to me. Those "CD of the month club" mailers with the sheet of perforated stamps you tore off, licked, and glued in place to select your choices? GOOD TIMES, my friends. Good times.

DAVE: *And no matter how many times you tried to cancel your subscription, the Wilson Phillips CDs kept right on coming.*

KORTNEY: *I'm sorry, did you say Wilson Phillips? You were a full-fledged adult man when they hit it big. I had no idea you were a fan of Wilson Phillips.*

DAVE: *Pfft. I've never even heard of Wilson Phillips. I said, I, Dave "Wilson," had my "fill of" those CD club mailers you were talking about. I have only ever listened to manly music for manly men.*

KORTNEY: *Right.*

Well, while our kids may not have the distinct pleasure of ordering CDs through the mail, they love getting an old-fashioned letter almost as much as their dad loved Chynna Phillips.

DAVE: *How did you know she was my favorite?*

KORTNEY: *I thought you'd never heard of Wilson Phillips.*

DAVE: *Damn it. You got me.*

KORTNEY: *I'm glad I got you. You're a big old sap like me.*

If there's one thing Dave and I have in common, it's that we're both sentimental fools. And we want our kids to know it. When the kids were younger and we had to travel, we'd mail them each a letter every day, so they'd know we were thinking of them.

DAVE: *We didn't actually mail them. You wrote them all before we left and then just left them in a stack and let your mom stick one in the mailbox each morning while she was babysitting.*

KORTNEY: *Well, I'm a sentimental fool who likes to plan ahead.*

Now that the kids are a little older, I still send them mail every once in a while, for no particular occasion, just to see them smile. Or, if I'm being realistic, I do it just to see Lennox smile, Sully blush, and Jett smirk at how embarrassing his parents are. (And I do actually have to mail them.) We'll tell the kids one awesome thing we've noticed about them, or comment on something they did that made us proud. I'll

try to sneak in a piece of mom wisdom—or one of Dave's life lessons—and always, always, we remind them, for the millionth time, that they are loved, unconditionally, by their dad and me.

The bottom line is this: there's something about writing a letter and dropping it in the mail that makes you slow down and reflect on how lucky and grateful you are. And regardless of whether the mail is met with a smile or an eye roll, the sender's reward is the same. It just feels good—and those feelings are what happy homes are made of.

CEILING FANS DON'T HAVE TO BE HIDEOUS

If you'd asked me 10 years ago for my opinion on ceiling fans, I would have told you to avoid them like the plague. If the blades themselves didn't kill you, the ugly would. But ever since a few lighting companies stepped up their game, bringing beautiful form to the highly functional (and eco-friendly) indoor fan, I've changed camps. As someone who cares about the environment, I can't knock anything that improves air quality and is more energy efficient, but from a design standpoint, it's important to marry the return on your investment with something that enhances your home's aesthetic. Especially indoors. Generic ceiling fans on porches, back decks, and screened-in sunrooms get my stamp of approval, but interior spaces should have a little more style.

How Not to Blow It with the Ceiling Fan

The fan-and-light-fixture combo is a practical solution, but proceed with caution. A modern fan blade combined with a faux-crystal chandelier can look like Liberace hanging from a helicopter.

Don't overdo it. If the blades have a unique design, keep the light fixture super simple. If the fixture is fancy, let the blades blend into the background.

Don't yank your own chain. Who wants to stand on tiptoe to turn on a fan? Not only are pull cords inconvenient to reach (especially for short-statured persons such as myself), they're

just plain ugly. If at all possible, hardwire your fans so they can be turned on with a traditional light switch.

Buy new. Ceiling fans are somewhat complicated structures with a combination of materials, which means they don't lend themselves to the DIY treatment. Painting an old ceiling fan is a lot of work, and unless you're careful to mask off the metal hardware with tape and match the fan's finish, the result is likely to disappoint you. If you want a unique and low-cost light fixture, spray-paint an old brass chandelier in a bold color and leave the fan out of it.

GIVE YOURSELF (AND OTHERS) PERMISSION TO VENT

——

I try to keep it pretty upbeat on social media—but sometimes a girl's just got to rant. The first time I ever let it rip on Instagram, I'd had what felt like an impossibly bad day. Everything that could have gone wrong did. And to top it all off, everyone around me was acting so ugly (that's a Southern term for "rude as hell") I wanted to curl up under the covers and refuse to come out until the universe reset itself. I fired off a hundred or so words of frustration, hit post, and walked away.

Then I panicked. *Who am I to complain? I've got it so good, I should just keep my mouth shut. Or, better yet, keep it open with a big toothy grin, so no one can call me ungrateful.* Before I could take the post down, though, I noticed there were more comments than usual.

And they weren't angry or eye-rolling. They were loving and supportive. And I'm not going to lie: more than one of them made me cry because of how kind they were.

Not only did commenters give me permission to vent, they *thanked me* for it. They shared similar stories of frustration or hardship, and rather than the whole thing devolving into a pity party, we started to lift each other up. It made me think about the expression "misery loves company" in a whole new way.

Loneliness is at the root of so much of our suffering. Even if loneliness is not the cause of our suffering, it's almost always the result. Negative experiences are incredibly isolating. We retreat into our own heads and try to wrestle with the mental gremlins alone. But when we share our burdens openly and honestly, they become lighter in the sharing.

Of course, there's a difference between occasional venting and *incessant whining*.

DAVE: *Allow our children to demonstrate.*

No one likes a whiner, I know. I try to make gratitude my default emotion, and on most days, my blessings far outweigh my grievances.

DAVE: *Unless a server sticks their fingers in your water glass when carrying it to the table, in which case all bets are off.*

KORTNEY: *Ugh, yes. That is hands down my biggest pet peeve. Total meal breaker.*

Though I probably wouldn't complain about it on Instagram.

DAVE: *Instagram is too fleeting. Better to mention it in a printed book. I hope our future waiters and waitresses are paying attention.*

Long story short: I appreciate everyone—from the neighbors next door to friends online I've never met—who supports us in our best and worst moments. So much. And I want to encourage everyone to extend the same kindness to one other. Being human is hard, but so much less so when we share the load.

MARRY HIM AGAIN

———

I knew about one year into our relationship that I wanted to be with Dave for the long haul. It took Dave another three years to get to the same place.

DAVE: *I'm a slow learner.*

Four years into our relationship, and completely out of the blue, he broke up with me *again*, saying he wasn't sure he wanted to get married at all. To anyone. He wasn't sure if he wanted kids. At all. With anyone.

DAVE: *We were kind of broke at that point. And there were days when I wasn't sure I wanted to put on pants. At all. For anyone. I was in love with this beautiful, ambitious woman, and frankly, it scared the sh*t out of me.*

I was devastated. The breakup made no sense. I thought we were on track. Our dreams and goals were aligned. We loved music. We loved each other. We were in this together. There was no plan B for me.

A week later, I was in the studio recording when I had an epiphany. Marriage or not, Dave

and I were meant to be together. I called him, ugly crying, and told him I wasn't going anywhere. If he wasn't ready for marriage now, or ever, I was okay with that.

Two weeks later, he proposed.

Three months later, we got married.

DAVE: *It was a very short engagement.*

KORTNEY: *I wanted to get my hooks into you for good.*

The wedding was a family-and-close-friends affair at Casa Loma, a castle in Toronto that is an extremely popular wedding venue. They had a last-minute cancellation, and we seized it. I wanted an all-white wedding (just my sisters and me in the wedding party), with green on the tables, and nice, simple food. Just me, and Dave, and the people we loved. No drama. As type A as I am in most other circumstances, I turned the majority of the planning over to my mother and she pulled it off without a hitch. The evening ended with Dave and I singing together at a grand piano with all of our family and friends alongside us. It was perfection, and if I had to do it over again, I wouldn't change a single thing.

DAVE: *Neither would I. But I did have to do it over again. Three times, in fact.*

It's true. Dave and I have renewed our vows three times since our wedding day: in Mexico, Niagara Falls, and Panama.

DAVE: *Marriage is highly addictive.*

KORTNEY: *And you are a sucker for romance. Even more so than I am. Not that I'm complaining.*

The last time we renewed our vows was after Dave re-proposed to me onstage in front of thousands of people in Northern Ontario. We had been singing together for a few years at this point and had recently signed a deal with Sony Music Canada. This was our first official show together as The Wilsons, and halfway through the set, the band started playing a song I didn't know. I completely panicked. Like, eyes popping, armpits sweating, panic. And then Dave started singing to me, a new song he'd written called "Marry Me Again." At the end, he got

down on one knee, presented me with a giant dollar-store diamond, and asked me to marry him again.

I was completely floored.

DAVE: *Davey did good on that one.*

KORTNEY: *You really did.*

And not only did the crowd go crazy for this moment, they wanted to get their hands on the song. Dave had never planned on recording it.

He'd written it for me. But the demand was there, so he rewrote the verses to suit a wider audience and we ended up recording it as our first single and shooting the video for it in Cuba.

DAVE: *That was a good time.*

KORTNEY: *Except that one time, in the freezing-cold water, when it wasn't.*

In the very last shot of that video, Dave and I are standing in the ocean. It's gorgeous and romantic and the sun is sparkling over the water. And behind the scenes, Dave and I were fighting like feral cats because he'd stayed up way too late the night before, when we had an early call time. He was looking a little rough, and I was not happy.

DAVE: *You were more than not happy. You were rabid.*

KORTNEY: *I'm a professional.*

DAVE: *And I am a simple caveman. I thought we'd established that.*

So there we were, waist-deep in water with the director, the videographer, the makeup artist, and someone holding a speaker so we could sync our lips with the music, and every time they told us to kiss, we would look at each other in disgust.

DAVE: *How many takes was it before you started liking me again?*

KORTNEY: *We got there before the sun went down. Which is all that matters, right?*

I know there are people who don't "believe" in renewing marriage vows. They'll say it's silly because the whole point of marriage is that marriage is forever.

DAVE: *Perhaps those people have never smelled their marriage's expiration date like I did while we were shooting "Marry Me Again."*

KORTNEY: *It was a little ironic.*

I love that we've renewed our vows. I love that we can acknowledge that marriage is an ongoing process, with ups and downs. Every day—whether we say it or not—we're renewing our vows to each other. So we might as well celebrate.

DAVE WILSON MASTER CLASS
HOLD YOUR MEMORIES CLOSE

———

Kortney and I have very different philosophies when it comes to the keepsakes from our pasts. I like to *keep* these items, because they are called *keepsakes*. The instructions are *written into the word*. Kortney, on the other hand, likes to dispose of these items because she is an authoritarian clutter buster who believes memories look neater stored in the California Closets of our *minds*.

KORTNEY: *Not true! I let you keep the secret stash of old love letters you have up in the attic.*

DAVE: *Well, for starters, the thing about a "secret" stash is that no one but me knows it's there. Which is clearly not the case here.*

KORTNEY: *I'm fine with it. I was just curious why you keep them.*

DAVE: *I keep them because they're my memories and memories have a shelf life.*

KORTNEY: *Do you ever take them off the shelf and read them?*

DAVE: *Never. I go back and read the actual secret stash that's in my dad's attic. The stash in our attic is a decoy stash to distract my nosy wife.*

KORTNEY: *Is the picture of your ex-girlfriend in the box in the top of your closet a decoy picture?*

DAVE: *Is the footage of us hosting Masters of Flip the real footage, or did you hire a stunt devil to fill in while you were at home rifling through all of my stuff?*

KORTNEY: *Did you say "stunt devil"?*

DAVE: *I said "stunt double."*

KORTNEY: *I'm pretty sure you said "stunt devil." And stop trying to make this about me! Dave, seriously. I don't mind that you keep letters and pictures from past girl-friends. I am secure enough in myself and our relationship to know that those old letters are nothing more than memories.*

DAVE: *You know, every time I look at those old letters, I think about how lucky I am to be married to you.*

KORTNEY: *I thought you said you never go back and look at them.*

DAVE: *Stunt. Devil.*

KORTNEY: *Letters aside, since you were up in the attic recently, you probably noticed it could use a little spring clean-ing. Why don't you go do that while I shine my pitchfork?*

TRADITIONS ARE NOT THE BOSS OF YOU

Traditions are *personal*. They exist to bring people together and foster connections. So if hosting a holiday dinner every year makes you want to run screaming for the hills, maybe it's time to stop hosting that holiday dinner. I know that may be easier said than done. Family can be tough terrain to navigate. But if I could have my wish, it would be for people to feel empowered to design their traditions the same way they design their homes: to fit the way they live and make them feel happy and at ease. That's why I've never been one to carry on traditions for tradition's sake. My preference is to keep what works, tweak what doesn't, and make up whatever I think is missing.

FRIENDSGIVING

For me, Thanksgiving falls into the keeper category. I love it so much I celebrate it twice. The fact that I have dual citizenship keeps me from looking like a Thanksgiving crazy-lady, but I'm not convinced an all-American or all-Canadian Kortney could resist two Thanksgivings either. I have *a lot* to be thankful for.

In October we celebrate Canadian Thanksgiving back home with family if at all possible. And I must admit I'm *very* glad my mom carries on with the traditional Thanksgiving fare I loved as a kid. (But I only love it because *she* loves it. Otherwise I'd say, "Out with the old, in with the new.") In November we celebrate American Thanksgiving, Southern style. Turkey, stuffing, casseroles upon casseroles (these are how Southern women sneak vegetables into unsuspecting men, by the way), and cornbread made in a cast-iron skillet, instead of rolls. Since our extended family is far away, and the same holds true for so many of our Nashville friends, we invite our nearest and dearest "framily" members for a big sit-down meal, followed by a take-no-prisoners game of Catch Phrase. We've dubbed this holiday "Friendsgiving."

THE UNHAUNTED HOUSE PARTY

East Nashville loves Halloween the way New Orleans loves Mardi Gras. People go crazy with decorations, the city shuts down our major through streets (including the one we live on),

and kids and families come out in *droves*. We have to take shifts handing out candy, because the stream of trick-or-treaters is nonstop all night long. In fact, I finally had to cap our candy budget at three thousand pieces, which sounds like a lot—but we run out *every single year*.

While the skeletons and ghouls and undead walk the neighborhood, we host a decidedly unhaunted house party where the grown-ups can flex their funny bones a bit. The costumes are hilarious. The crockpot is full of chili. And there are usually two kinds of soup simmering on the stove.

And then there's *Dave* waddling around the kitchen in his professional-grade Donald Duck costume.

DAVE: *I don't waddle. I strut with style and conviction.*

The year Jett was born, I decided it was time for Dave and I to up our costume game. I stalked an online costume warehouse for several weeks *after* Halloween until I scored us three Disney character costumes on clearance. Jett made a precious Winnie-the-Pooh the next year, and I was an extremely effeminate Aladdin (it was the only costume they had left in my size), but Dave's Donald Duck suit was a tour de force. So much so that he's worn it every Halloween since. Our trick-or-treaters have no clue who Dave and Kortney Wilson are, but they sure know where "the duck guy" lives.

DAVE: *They also know the duck guy's wife buys three thousand pieces of candy every year, which might have something to do with the steady traffic.*

THE HERITAGE POTLUCK

In the fall of 2017, my political angst had reached full gestation and I was on the verge of exploding. My adopted country was embroiled in so much ugliness, division, and hate, it pained me to follow the news—and it pained me *not* to. I firmly believe that challenging times call for us to pay more attention, not less. And that includes drawing your loved ones close and paying more attention to each other, which is how the Heritage Potluck was born. Granted, this party wasn't meant to be a political act; it was more of a much-needed love fest and a reminder that hardly any of us so-called Americans are really natives of this country.

On a Wednesday night, I emailed some friends:

Heritage Potluck.
This Saturday.
Our House.
6 p.m.
Bring a dish that celebrates your heritage.
And, if you'd like to, bring a friend.

DAVE: *And "bring a friend" they did.*

KORTNEY: *It was amazing.*

What started out as an intimate gathering turned into 80-plus people and a kitchen *covered* in extraordinary cuisine from all over the world. The weather was exceptionally beautiful, and the crowd spilled out onto our back patio, where we had live music all night long.

A sidebar about East Nashville: Almost *everyone* we know here is musical, so we can have amazing live music without having to hire a band. One by one, our guests got up and performed their favorite songs, while we piled our plates with everything from dim sum to baloney sandwiches (courtesy of a friend who proudly claims her heritage as "100 percent redneck").

At the risk of sounding like a sap, this night made me feel *all the feelings*. Like the world was still good, and still something to celebrate. That's a feeling I want to relive year after year.

NOITIDART (THAT'S "TRADITION" SPELLED BACKWARDS)

If there's a holiday you hate (for me, that would be Valentine's Day), turn it into something you love. Women celebrating women on Galentine's Day (that's on February 13, if you haven't heard) is *exactly* what I'm talking about. There's also the option to (gasp!) *ignore a holiday altogether*. No calendar is the boss of you.

If carrying on a tradition brings you joy, *have at it*, but the minute it becomes a burden or something you dread or resent, consider it time to change it up, or let it go.

SAVE YOUR SAMPLES!

Dave and I travel a ton, so I've taken to saving the tiny toiletries from the different hotels where we've stayed. To be clear, we are not stealing these items from the housekeeping cart (though I've witnessed others doing this on countless occasions); we're simply holding on to the ones we're given during our stay. And they've come in mighty handy.

When guests come to stay with us, I'll fill a tall vase or pretty basket with miniature shampoos and conditioners, lotions, toothpaste, mouthwash, etc., and set it out in the guest room. It also makes a great backup for when you run out of some crucial item and realize it's too late to make a shopping run.

If you get your friends on the sample-saving train, you could even consider combining your stash and giving it to a charity, like a homeless shelter. The kids and I have done this a few times with our friends over the years, and it's a fun way to spread some love.

LOVE YOUR LAUNDRY (ROOM)

I don't love doing laundry, but I do love our laundry room. And this makes a big difference when it comes to common household chores. Never put a chore you're inclined to avoid in a *room* you want to avoid. It's that simple. The laundry room should be kept clean, just like the clothes you wash there.

I've always been baffled by people who have "laundry day." At our house, every day is laundry day. As soon as there's enough for a load, in (and out) it goes. Why wait and commit yourself to an entire day of dirty underwear? You can design your week better than that.

The laundry room is ideal when it's just that—a room. Having room for storage is priceless, as is being able do everything in one space (washing, drying, ironing, and folding). But if you don't have a dedicated laundry room, have no fear; we have storage solutions for you too.

Tips to Love Your Laundry Room on a Dime

- **Paint it a fun color.** Choose something that makes you smile (laundry typically doesn't).

- **Or paint it white.** There's something about a clean white laundry room that I love. It matches the *feeling* of clean laundry, and you can easily paint over any spots or stains to keep it looking fresh.

- **No clutter.** Keep a small trash can close at hand for loose wrappers and dryer lint, and a small basket to collect all of the other stuff you find in pockets. Put a sign on the basket that says "Everything will be thrown out on Monday mornings, so if you're missing something, now's the time to look."

- **Build up and around your front loader.** I'm a big fan of the low front loaders, but you might consider building a platform that brings the units to waist level. Your back will thank you for it. They sell the stands with the units, but you can build them for a fraction of the cost and customize the size and color. Speaking of customizing, this is the perfect place to build custom shelving, right up to the ceiling. The idea is to utilize every square inch on the wall that holds

the appliances, leaving the other walls for organization.

- **Small space?** No problem. If a laundry closet is the card you've been dealt, place a shoe organizer on the inside of each of the French doors. On one side, place small laundry supplies like lint removers and stain sticks. On the other, miscellaneous unmatched socks and unclaimed change and lip balms.

- **Make a folding spot.** The alternative to raising the appliances is to keep them low and install an inexpensive piece of butcher block over the tops to create a folding spot. Premium plywood cut to size by your local hardware store can also work.

- **Reunite single socks.** No one knows where the single socks go. It's one of life's most enduring mysteries. One of the cutest things I've seen online was a piece of wood with little hooks at the bottom to hold socks. The sign read "Single and Looking for a Mate." Practical and adorable.

- **Sort your stuff.** If you're not sorting your laundry, now's the time to start. Your clothes will look so much better for so much longer. In our house, we have a basket for whites, one for colors, and a third for wash rags (which we use in abundance for cleaning, in order to cut down on paper towels).

HANG ORNAMENTS TO SUIT THE SEASON

———

When it comes to holiday decor, I subscribe to the "less is more" philosophy.

DAVE: *Except at Halloween, when more is more, and it's still never enough.*

KORTNEY: *When it comes to candy, yes. But even on Halloween, you still won't see me covering the house in cobwebs and candy corn.*

DAVE: *If memory serves me, there is always a nine-foot inflatable spider living on our front lawn the entire month of October.*

KORTNEY: *Doris? She's not a decoration. She's family.*

DAVE: *Ah. My mistake. Carry on.*

As much as I love the holidays (well, except Valentine's Day), I want to *celebrate* them, not *succumb* to them. And that means exercising some restraint when it comes to seasonal decor.

Especially in the kitchen, which gets tons of traffic and tends to be the hub of our holiday celebrations. The more utilitarian the room, the less "decked out" I like it to be. That said, I do love for the kitchen to have a tiny touch of holiday flair. And for that, the chandelier is ideal.

It is now a family tradition to collect and hang ornaments that suit the season. Easter eggs in spring, homemade Halloween ghosts and bats in October, treasured Christmas ornaments in December. And while I'm not a fan of Valentine's Day, I've been known to hang a heart or two to show some love between New Year's and Mardi Gras.

What I love about the chandelier is that it's festive, not festooned, and it's up and out of harm's way, giving the kitchen a seasonal mini makeover—instead of a seasonal *takeover*. If you don't have a chandelier, doorways are another great place to add seasonal flair. For Mardi Gras, for example, you might hang beads with small tacks (not floor to ceiling like a bunch of love beads—just a few short strands overhead—like Mardi Gras mistletoe).

FRAME THE FRIDGE

S ad fact: refrigerators are ugly. If you happen to be house hunting, you might even notice that the fridge is missing from homes on the market. It's worth asking yourself why. Often it's because the refrigerator hookup was installed in the most awkward and unsightly location possible. When I walk into a newly renovated home and the refrigerator is missing, that empty space is a big red flag that the builder forgot to factor in the fridge when designing the open-concept kitchen. If all of the other appliances are there, there's a good chance the fridge was removed because it was sticking out like a sore thumb. A refrigerator with no walls or cabinetry on either side will shrink an open-concept kitchen faster than you can say "Frigidaire." Why? Because standard cabinets are 24 inches (60 centimeters) deep, and a standard fridge is 30 inches (75 centimeters). And that's with the doors closed.

My point? Plan ahead. Careful consideration must be given to the fridge on the front end of every kitchen design. I will sometimes design entire kitchens around the fridge because of how clunky they can look if I don't.

How to Fix a Funky Fridge Situation

- **Rightsize it.** If you're stuck with a poorly positioned fridge and a renovation is not in the foreseeable future, consider a smaller appliance. I'd rather see you stick a secondary fridge in the garage or basement and have a cohesive kitchen design. We actually have a counter-depth refrigerator in our own home, and the smaller cubic footage forces us to shop more frequently, so we end up eating more fresh food and having less waste.

- **Frame it.** If the placement of your fridge is the problem, and one or both of its sides are exposed, consider custom cabinetry to frame it. A carpenter can do this for you fairly inexpensively, using particleboard that you can then paint—or butcher block, which looks gorgeous and isn't too pricey either. Use whatever budget you can muster to avoid having an un-flanked fridge.

- **Make it flush.** With built-in refrigerators, be sure that the fridge box (not including the door) is flush with the cabinet, so when you do open the door, it will swing freely.

- **Finish it.** Finish off the look of your kitchen by addressing the space above the fridge. Open shelving, custom cabinets, or even a really big basket will draw your eye upward and make the fridge area feel finished. Since it's not the most accessible space, I recommend storing nonessentials or items you use only on special occasions. We store our giant turkey roaster in that cabinet, since we only use it once a year.

DAVE: *Watching you climb up there and wrestle that thing down to ground level every year is one of my favorite Thanksgiving traditions. It's like when Santa arrives at the end of the big parade.*

KORTNEY: *Except this Santa is a five-foot-two vegetarian whose elves just stand there and laugh at her while she wrestles with the turkey roaster.*

DAVE: *It's TRADITION.*

BE READY TO FIND "THE ONE"

——

A home is the single largest investment you'll probably ever make, but if you're in a competitive market, you may only have one viewing and a matter of hours to "say YES to the house." That is *not* the time to start over-thinking. It's also not the time to panic and risk overpaying in the midst of a multiple-offer situation. That's why it's so important to set parameters for yourself in advance. I recommend making several lists before you venture out into the market:

A Trio of Lists

- **Must haves.** If you know you need three bedrooms, two living areas, and a master suite on the main level, go ahead and set it in stone. If you can't live without an accessible attic—or a finished basement—write

it down and decide right now you're not going to waver. Done. That way you're not tempted in the heat of the moment to bid on a house that falls short of your main criteria.

- **Love to haves.** This is your wish list. Maybe it's a formal dining room. Or a walk-out basement. Or a backyard pool or extra guest room. None of these is a deal breaker, but if a house has them *and* it meets your must-have criteria, that's a good sign it's a keeper.

- **Willing to pay more for.** These are the things on your wish list that you're willing to increase your budget for. You must be clear *how much more* you're willing to pay. If you're buying with a partner, making this decision in advance could save the two of you a heated discussion during a time that

My House Wish List

MUST HAVES - Non-negotiable!
- ❏ A guest bedroom for your mother-in-law
- ✓ A bathtub - or how else will I unwind?
- ❏ A grassy area for Skippy.

LOVE TO HAVE - But, ugh, I could give if I have to.
- ❏ An attached garage
- ❏ A walk-in closet
- ❏ A pool

WILLING TO PAY MORE FOR - I'll bite the bullet because it's THAT important to me.
- ❏ A house near the park
- ❏ A She-Shed
- ❏ Close to the ice cream store

should be fun and memorable. (Take it from one who knows.) Examples might be storage, a garage, additional acreage, or proximity to an ice cream store. Whatever it is, identify it early. Put a price tag on it. And stick to your guns.

Now, with all of that in mind, there is still something to be said for good old-fashioned intuition. When your main criteria have been met, have the confidence to trust your inner voice. How do you feel? Does this house feel like home? If you had to decide *right this*

second, would it be a yes or a no? If the little voice inside you is jumping up and down, clapping her hands, and screaming "YES YES YES," well, congratulations. You're ready to walk down the aisle—or through the front door, as it were. If a house meets all of your criteria and there's *still* a nagging voice in your head that something's not quite right, by all means honor that as well. I'll say it again and again: a home is personal. And you're the person who has to live there and love it. So go into the process prepared—and you'll be better prepared to give your inner voice the final word.

MAKE IT, OR FAKE IT

———

As human beings, we crave symmetry. We tend to rate facial beauty (especially women's faces) against a scale of symmetry. Much of what we find in nature is endowed with symmetry—bodies, flowers, leaves, shells, seeds, snowflakes. And because of that, these things feel purposeful, and not random. As if they were created *by design*.

So it makes perfect sense that designers strive for symmetry in the spaces we create. We fantasize about the rectangular room in which one half is the mirror image of the other. The door is centered on one wall; the windows are balanced and evenly placed. The chandelier is perfectly centered over the coffee table, with conversation sofas and matching chairs

radiating out like sunbeams. It's a beautiful daydream. But in reality, it never happens. And, frankly, it runs the risk of being a bit boring.

DAVE: *Right. I mean, does this symmetrical dream living room have two baby grand pianos? And two cupcake dispensers? It just feels like overkill.*

KORTNEY: *Which is why designers think in broader terms of balance.*

Symmetry is a kind of balance, but it's not the only kind. We like symmetry because it's easy—at least in theory. But in reality, asymmetrical balance is much more attainable. And a lot

more interesting. Instead of two identical sofas mirroring each other, you might balance the sofa with two matching chairs placed opposite it. While the sofa may be technically heavier, the visual weight of these objects is the same.

When I'm planning a room layout, I like to imagine that the room is on a scale that measures the visual weight of everything in it. This helps me determine whether the room is balanced or whether one side is considerably "heavier" than the other.

Let's say you have a grand piano on one side of your living room. It's likely a focal point. A large piece of art hanging opposite the piano will restore balance in the room, without diminishing the piano's power.

Another simple example is a home's front door. You'd be surprised how often the front door is not centered. If it's hanging a little to the left, I might put a chair to the right of it to restore the visual balance. It's not symmetrical, but it feels right. And the more you pay attention to visual balance, the easier it becomes to identify and adjust it.

True symmetry—where elements mirror one another—should feel natural, not forced. I tend to save it for the smaller touches, like lamps and end tables, or a sofa centered on a gorgeous rug, with matching throw pillows on either side.

FLOAT THE SOFA

———

Nothing makes my brain curdle like a giant room where all of the seating is pushed to the outskirts of the room, backing up to one or more walls. This is not a fifth-grade dance, with boys on one side and girls on the other; it's your living room! So let's mingle a little, shall we?

The first question you should ask yourself when arranging a room is this: What is the room's focal point? Is it a fireplace? A textured accent wall? A piece of art or a mounted television? Maybe it's a window with a stunning view. If the room doesn't *have* a natural focal point, create one, and build around it. Instead of placing the sofa on the largest wall, try placing it across from the focal point. Not *all-the-way-across-the-room* across, but facing it, at a reasonable distance. Then position your secondary seating (club chairs, love seat) in harmonious conversation-distance of the sofa.

Open floor plans are becoming increasingly popular, and in these spaces, which are deliberately *lacking* in walls, the sofa is what anchors the space and creates flow. I find it helpful to envision the room from above (a bird's-eye view, if you will) and think of the sofa as a Lego block. Set it several feet off a wall and you create a nice corridor behind it. Place it in the center of the room and you have a natural room divider. If the room is *extra* large, consider floating multiple sofas to create different areas of activity within the room. One for intimate conversation, perhaps, and one for larger groups to sit and enjoy a game. Any of these options can work if you're open to them—it's simply a matter of how you want to use the space. Just remember: your sofa is not a frightened teenager with its back up against the wall, surveying a crowded dance floor.

If you don't love the look of your sofa back, a console table is a nice touch that makes the placement of the sofa feel smart and deliberate. If your room is too small to float the sofa and have plenty of room to walk around it, I *still* recommend floating the sofa a bit off the wall and sliding a console table behind it. It's a great place to display photographs and other items of significance and it gives the room a feeling of greater depth.

TREAT A KID LIKE
AN ONLY CHILD

⎯

Whether or not you're a parent, I hope you have the chance to connect with a special kid, one-on-one. It really is medicine for the soul. Yours—and theirs. Of course, the more kids you have, the harder it can be to give them your undivided attention. I come from a family of six, and the rare times I spent one-on-one with my mom or dad are ingrained in my memory forever. Dave and I want the same for our kids, which is why, in addition to the little moments we carve out here and there, we do some deliberate planning to ensure each kid gets some extended only-kid time every year.

THE BIRTHDAY DATE

On each of our children's birthdays, Dave and I take them out of school for a special meal. It's become a tradition for us to tell them their birth story, and I find it so sweet and funny that they never get tired of hearing it. Every year, they want to know some new detail—like what I ate when I was pregnant (pickles and raw red bell peppers), or what they wore, or how I felt on the first day we brought them home. We tell them how Daddy forgot to charge the video camera when Jett was born and did everything in his power to not repeat that performance with Sully.

DAVE: *The camera was charged, but when I saw Sully's head . . .*

KORTNEY: *You shot a two-hour video of the delivery room ceiling.*

DAVE: *It was a really big head.*

It's funny: these dates are almost awkward at first—because it casts the kid in a different role. They start to tell you things that they wouldn't think to say with their siblings nearby, and I realize over and over again how important it is for them to be *seen*, apart from everyone else.

THE GIFT OF A TRIP

We've seriously scaled back on the gift giving as the kids have grown. Instead of toys or clothes or miscellaneous stuff, we want to give them experiences. And we want to give them experiences that they can have all to

themselves, one-on-one trips with Dave or me, to someplace they've never been. We gave each kid a trip for Christmas this year, and they each said they want to make it a standing tradition. And it doesn't have to be a trip to someplace exotic or far-flung! A day trip or outing to a new part of town could do just the trick.

I took Lennox to Dallas and Jett to New York City. Dave took Sully to Boston. There's such rich history in that city; I wanted them to have that quintessential New England sightseeing experience.

DAVE: *Yes. Sightseeing. We saw many, many sights.*

KORTNEY: *Why are you talking like that?*

DAVE: *Talking like what? I was just seeing in my mind's eye the sights we saw when we went sightseeing. So many historical sights to see.*

KORTNEY: *Dave . . .*

DAVE: *I'm sorry! We got distracted! By the pizza and the drinks and the other foods.*

KORTNEY: *You sent me pictures every day.*

DAVE: *Those were real.*

KORTNEY: *But you didn't see those sights?*

DAVE: *We saw them. We just didn't SEE them.*

KORTNEY: *But you took pictures of them?*

DAVE: *Yes. All of them. In two hours. Before we even checked into the hotel. So we would have a stockpile of sightseeing pictures to send you while we were eating the pizza and the other foods.*

KORTNEY: *You've got to be kidding.*

DAVE: *We were making memories!*

While it wouldn't have killed them to actually *walk* the Freedom Trail, having the freedom to just be guys together was probably worth more than any sight they could have seen. And Lennox will remember the mother-daughter manicure more than the Dallas Arboretum, and Jett will fondly recall buying some fancy sneakers in Times Square.

And it really doesn't matter what we *did*, does it? Just that we did it, one-on-one, together.

DAVE: *You handled that well.*

KORTNEY: *Thank you.*

DAVE WILSON MASTER CLASS
DON'T BE AFRAID TO THROW AWAY THE SCRIPT

———

People ask us all the time if we really flip houses. My blood pressure and I can attest that we actually do. We find the houses. We buy the houses. We fix up the houses. Sometimes we screw up the houses and have to fix them up again. And then we have to *sell* the houses. It's terrifying.

Maybe "terrifying" is the wrong word, but the stakes are high, there's no safety net, and Kortney and I are under a lot of pressure to make a lot of smart decisions in a very short period of time. This requires a lot of planning, a lot of organization, and unwavering attention to detail. Lucky for Kortney, I'm terrible at all three.

So, in conclusion, I have no idea what I'm doing here, doling out life advice to people who are probably way smarter, more organized, and detail oriented than I am. Thank you for your time, and to all a good night.

KORTNEY: *Dave, this tip is supposed to be about throwing away the script.*

You're right. Case in point. We had a plan, and I forgot the plan.

DAVE: *Thank you, Kortney, for keeping me alive all these years.*

KORTNEY: *The pleasure is all mine.*

So! Throwing away the script! *That* is something I can get behind. In fact, if there is one thing I, Dave Wilson, am exceptionally good at, it's having no idea what's going to happen next.

Winging It for the Win

When Sully and I took our father-son trip over the holidays, Kortney had big plans for us. She purchased our flights and reserved our hotel rooms in Boston, knowing that if she left it up to me, we'd stay at the Nashville Airport Marriott and watch movies and play video games all week. (With Sully, you're guaranteed a good time no matter where you go. He's just that kind of kid. Easy, breezy, and deserving of a mother with superior planning skills.) Fortunately, Kortney is such a mother, and when we landed in Boston, we were glad we made it.

Our only big plan was to eat *all* of the Italian food, which Boston is known for. Pizza, pasta, calzones, cannoli, the works. Then the cab dropped us off at our hotel, right smack in the middle of Chinatown.

Chinese food it is! All day, every day, we ate our fill of Chinese and didn't think twice about the Italian food we were missing. We were rebels without calzones.

At one point along the way, we did manage to grab a couple slices (delicious!), only to walk out of the pizza parlor and see a hawk swoop down, grab a squirrel, and eat it right in front of us. This was disappointing. And unappetizing. But Sully, my little sage, said, "It's okay, Dad. These things are just part of life." You're right, Sully. Sometimes squirrels get murdered while you're eating pizza in Boston. Easy come, easy go.

Maps Are for Amateurs

Next up, we decided to tackle public transit. We would take the subway to the ferry, ride the ferry around Boston Harbor, and take the subway back again. That was the extent of our plan.

We hopped on the subway and rode 20 minutes in the wrong direction. When we realized our mistake, we asked a stranger for directions and boarded a different subway, headed for our destination. If either of us had listened to the kind stranger, we might have made it there, but why listen when you can just *think you're listening*? It requires so much less brain space. For 40 minutes we rode the subway, laughing and chatting, and when it finally came to a stop, we were psyched.

We had made it!

We were going on a ferry ride.

We were right back where we'd started.

Chinese food and a movie at the hotel it is, kid.

I don't think Sully and I have ever laughed as hard as we did that day. We rode a subway, going nowhere. We finally ate some pizza. We watched a squirrel's untimely demise. We ate more Chinese food. And we realized just how much we enjoy each other's company.

Would we have had just as much fun seeing museums and monuments? Maybe. But I don't know. Every time I look back on this unscripted trip with my kid, I think I couldn't have planned it better.

MAKE A LIST

Maybe you can relate to this. You've had a long day. You're physically exhausted and you can barely keep your eyes open. You crawl into bed, switch off the light, and your brain decides that now would be a perfect time to start evaluating your past performance as a human being and predicting all of the ways you're likely to fail in the future. I mean, why not? You're just *lying there*. Why not do something productive?

MY BRAIN: *You really screwed the pooch on getting Jett to school on time this morning, Kort. If you do that again tomorrow, he will miss his geography test, which counts as 25 percent of his grade, and he can pretty much kiss the Ivy League goodbye.*

ME: *I'm not going to be late tomorrow. I set the alarm.*

MY BRAIN: *Speaking of alarms, did you*

order the security system for the rental property on Anderson Street? Someone is probably robbing your tenants at gunpoint as we speak.*

ME: *Okay. First of all, "we" are not speaking. You are speaking, and I am trying to fall asleep. So knock it off.*

MY BRAIN: *I'm just trying to help you stay on top of things. There's no need to be rude. Speaking of rude, can you believe the tone that woman took with you in that email earlier today? OUTRAGEOUS. Are you going to respond to that or let it go?*

ME: *I'm not going to respond to her. I'm just going to stick to my guns.*

MY BRAIN: *Speaking of guns, you need to contact your senators and tell them to vote no on that weapons legislation.*

It's out of control. And the only way I can get my brain to settle down is to get its nagging voice out of my head and onto the page, as quickly as possible. I keep a notepad and pen in my nightstand for this very reason, and it has saved me many sleepless hours.

- *Jett—geography test*
- *Security system, Anderson Street*
- *Respond to crazy lady's email (or don't)*
- *Contact senators re: gun control!*
- *Get doctor to prescribe sleeping pills*

I'm only kidding about that last one, but you get the idea. You want your bedroom to be a peaceful sanctuary, but your brain doesn't always get the memo. Making a notepad part of your bedroom decor might be the best design decision you'll ever make.

DAVE WILSON MASTER CLASS
YOU CAN DUET

—

Shortly after Kortney and I stopped pursuing solo careers and started singing together, we auditioned for a reality TV show called *Can You Duet?* Created by the same people who brought the world *American Idol*, the show's goal was to discover the next big country duo. We submitted an audition tape of the two of us singing a song I'd written called "Still Got Time for You," and within a week, we got a call from the show's producers, saying they loved us, they loved the song, and they wanted to meet us in person to learn more about our "backstory."

This was it, we thought.

We have a "backstory" now. Next stop, the American dream.

KORTNEY: *We were feeling pretty confident. Like it was meant to be.*

DAVE: *All those hours doing Tae Bo in front of the TV were finally starting to make sense.*

Kortney had us on a rigorous diet and workout regimen. We were eating like birds, running like lions, and caring for our precious voices like Céline Dion. We were in the best shape of our lives, and now we were going to be famous. We were sure of it.

On the day of our on-camera audition, I let Kortney give me a mud-mask facial for good luck. We were ready. Our pores were ready.

We would be auditioning for a panel of judges at the Wildhorse Saloon near lower Broadway. And while it was technically the first audition, the production team had already come to our house and filmed footage of us for a future episode, so we were confident we'd make it through.

We got to the Wildhorse and signed in along with 400 other hopefuls awaiting their shot at stardom. But it didn't faze us.

KORTNEY: *We felt like industry veterans at this point. We'd had record deals.*

DAVE: *We had a backstory!*

KORTNEY: *We just had to go in there and sing our hearts out for the judges, so we could move through to the next round.*

DAVE: *And then the top 10.*

KORTNEY: *And probably the final two.*

DAVE: *Did I mention we were confident?*

Two by two, they called teams in to audition for the panel behind closed doors. When our number was called, the producers asked how we were feeling.

KORTNEY: *We were nervous, but confident.*

Don't be afraid to play up the nerves, the producers said. It's endearing. It makes you seem real.

KORTNEY: *I was nervous—as any person would be. But it wasn't my style to show it. Especially not to the judges.*

DAVE: *But you could take direction.*

KORTNEY: *I could. And I did.*

We sang our first song and felt great about it. The judges were engaged and nodding along. Then halfway through our second song, they stopped us. Kortney, as if on cue, laughed a little and said, "Hoo. I'm nervous."

And the judges issued their verdict.

KORTNEY: *Do you remember exactly what they said?*

DAVE: *No. But I remember the gist. "I didn't like what you did there. The vocal blend was off."*

KORTNEY: *And then the clincher . . .*

DAVE: *"You seem really nervous."*

KORTNEY: *My heart dropped.*

The judges thought we were cute.

KORTNEY: *Cute.*

But we needed more time to develop and— wait for it—*find our confidence.*

Twenty years later, it feels like just another embarrassing footnote, but that moment was excruciating.

KORTNEY: *Because we were so confident.*

It had never occurred to us that we would be rejected that day. So to be rejected, in large part for not having enough confidence, was just more than our cute little brains could handle.

KORTNEY: *It was humiliating. I felt like such an idiot for believing we had this in the bag, when now here I was digging through my actual bag, looking for a tissue, so I could wipe my stupid crying face.*

Driving home that afternoon, I looked over at my beautiful, sobbing wife and said, "Do you want to do Tae Bo later?"

KORTNEY: *I remember that. You made me laugh.*

DAVE: *And then I made you order McDonald's.*

For the next 24 hours, we did nothing but watch movies and eat fast food and feel sorry for ourselves. There was no Tae Bo. No talk of music. No plotting our next move. Just mourning our loss and crushing burgers and fries and frozen dairy desserts. Together.

KORTNEY: *Like best friends do.*

The judges said we couldn't duet. But we knew we could. And we did. And we still do.

CHILL-O ON THE PILLOWS

Decorative pillows are a fun and effective way to add color to a neutral space or to balance a large swath of color—like a red accent wall—with smaller pops of that same color throughout a room. It's a lot of fun to mix and match different patterns and textures, and shapes and sizes, and I encourage it—but you must exercise some restraint and remember that the furniture's function comes first. If your sofa is sporting so many pillows there's no place to sit, you've gone too far. Or as my teenager would say, "You need to chill." So. We've established that it's best not to overdo it. Let's talk about how not to *underdo it*. There is nothing sadder than two flimsy little pillows trying (and failing) to frame a sofa.

DAVE: *I'm pretty sure I just watched a Lifetime movie about this. Cried my eyes out. I just wanted the pillows to be successful, you know?*

KORTNEY: *Nice.*

If you want your pillows to be successful, remember these two things: first, their role is to decorate, not dominate, and second, every pillow needs a buddy by its side.

DAVE: *Teamwork makes the dream work!*

KORTNEY: *Yes. Yes, it does.*

DAVE WILSON MASTER CLASS
KNOW WHEN NOT TO DIY

———

Like many people, Kortney has always loved getting massages. And in the early days of our romance, a massage was one of the few gifts I could actually afford to give her, so I gave her a lot of them.

KORTNEY: *Those were good times.*

They were also hungry times. I was working as the world's worst waiter, with the world's crappiest car (it didn't lock), and I wondered if we'd ever get our heads above water. But as long as Kortney got her massages, she was happy . . .

For our first Christmas together, I wanted to do something really special, something that would show not just how much I loved her, but how much I *understood* her. So I hatched a plan to *build* her her very own massage table.

KORTNEY: *It was the sweetest thing anyone had ever made me.*

DAVE: *It was also the most poorly constructed thing anyone had ever made you.*

A carpenter I was not. But what I lacked in skill, I *more* than made up for with stupidity. I drove all over the city collecting materials to build this table. I spent about $150 on wood and foam and vinyl, which was an astronomical amount of money for us at the time.

KORTNEY: *But you were determined.*

DAVE: *And let's not forget stupid!*

To keep this gift a surprise, I was storing all of the materials in the back of my car. My rickety stick shift (Volkswagen) that, in case you've forgotten, *did not lock.*

KORTNEY: *This part is so sad.*

DAVE: *The part where all my materials get stolen? Or the part where I spend another $150 to replace them? Because to me, that's the heartbreaker.*

For reasons that are still unclear to me, it never crossed my mind that I could *buy* a massage table for little more than the cost of materials. I had in my head that the only way to give Kortney this gift was to make it myself. So, I'm out in the garage hammering and bolting this thing together, and I can't afford a saw to cut it down when I bring it inside and realize it takes up the entire length of our living room.

KORTNEY: *It was massive.*

DAVE: *It was. But the way I'd built it, the legs could fold up underneath it and we could store it—at least somewhat—out of sight. Until . . .*

KORTNEY: *Until . . .*

Christmas morning comes along and I finally unveil my masterpiece. It is *enormous* and *unsightly* and Kortney is trying so hard to be enthusiastic about this monstrosity in the middle of our living room. She gamely hops up on the table and sticks her head through the little face hole.

KORTNEY: *Like, all the way through.*

DAVE: *Yes, because the face hole was huge. I'd just told the guy at the hardware store to cut a head-sized hole. I didn't get real specific about whose head.*

So we get a bunch of towels and duct tape and craft a smaller face hole for Kortney, and she hops back up on the table, sticks her head through the ring of duct tape and towels, and . . .

KORTNEY: *And I'm trying really hard to relax . . .*

And the legs give out.

KORTNEY: *I go crashing to the floor.*

My *soul* goes crashing to the floor.

KORTNEY: *It was a good 10 seconds before you could even bring yourself to ask me if I was okay. Which I was. It was hilarious.*

DAVE: *It was so not hilarious.*

But instead of just giving up on this thing,

I decided to reattach and reinforce the legs so they wouldn't fold. So they *couldn't* fold. The massage table was now a permanent fixture in our living room.

KORTNEY: *And I just had to get over it.*

DAVE: *Which pained you.*

KORTNEY: *It did. But you gave me so many massages to make up for it, I almost didn't mind. Those massages got me through my first pregnancy.*

And for her first Mother's Day, I went out and bought her a real massage table. One that folds up and stores neatly in a closet.

KORTNEY: *Which reminds me, we need to use it more. I keep forgetting it's there.*

DAVE: *We could always put it in the living room. For old time's sake.*

KORTNEY: *I think my style's evolved too much since then.*

Fortunately, my style has evolved since then too. And my style is to never make something I could more easily, and *way* more affordably, buy.

GO FOR THE GOLD
(AND THE SILVER)

———

There are certain "rules" that weasel their way into your brain, and once they take hold, it's almost impossible to break them. Mixing metals was one of those rules for me. Somewhere along the line, it was ingrained in me that wearing silver and gold jewelry at the same time was a sin on par with wearing white after Labor Day.

DAVE: *Are you sure wearing white after Labor Day is still a sin?*

KORTNEY: *Actually, no. Which is kind of my point. These rules are hard to shake.*

I remember standing frozen at the bathroom mirror, wearing gold hoops and a silver statement necklace and wondering if the world would stop spinning on its axis if I went out of the house that way.

DAVE: *This story is a real nail-biter. Tell us what happened! Tell us what happened!*

I got over it. The earrings and necklace looked good together. I knew it instinctively, but I still had to overrule my inner rule follower.

Lucky for all of us, design rules aren't nearly as rigid as they once were. And mixing metals is not only accepted, it's encouraged. Hardware, light fixtures, home decor, and furniture are often a mixed bag of silver and gold. The key is to make it look harmonious, not haphazard—and there are a couple of tricks to this.

Mixing Metals for the Win

When you go for the gold and silver, decide which one will be dominant. When I talk about gold and silver, I'm really referring to the color values, not necessarily the metals themselves. Whether it's gold, brass, bronze, or copper, these "gold" metals will give the room a warm tone; silver, pewter, chrome, and stainless steel are cool tones. One of these tones—gold or silver, warm or cool—should be the dominant palette, while the other plays a supporting role.

Strike a balance. While it's important to choose a dominant metal, you still have to be attentive to balance. If the entire room is done in copper, for example, a tiny little side table in chrome will feel like it doesn't belong. So sprinkle in a few other chrome pieces—a frame, a vase, or a decorative tray—to make it feel deliberate. Also, be sure to strike a spatial balance as well, distributing metals evenly throughout the space, so each tone appears in multiple places.

Combine finishes with care. There's more than one way to cook an egg—and way more than one way to finish metal. High polish, satin, brushed, hammered, antique, oil-rubbed, flat. So many choices! And when it comes to silver and gold, too many contrasting finishes tends to compete with one another. (This is not the case for black metals, which don't have the same reflective properties as silver and gold—so if you like a mix of finishes, black metals will give you more freedom to play.) Again, you want to choose a dominant finish and one or two accent finishes to bring visual interest and texture to the room. But no more than that.

Keep hardware uniform. Handles, pulls, and knobs should have a clean, cohesive look. Using the same metal throughout and selecting hardware from the same collection will do you right every time. If you feel the need to shake it up, try silver on the uppers and gold pulls on the lower drawers (in the same finish, of course).

Better yet, find hardware that has the metals interwoven in the design already.

The larger the room, the more room to play. This is not to say a small space can't have an eclectic mix of metals; just in keep in mind that metals—warm or cool—are reflective and require room to breathe so that they don't become visually overwhelming.

IS IT BLACK YOU LACK?

———

Black is an anchor. It works almost every-where—and in every style of design. Whether I'm painting an interior, refinishing furniture, choosing hardware, adding an end table, or hanging a light fixture, black never lets me down. In our living room, for example, we have a mix of tones and textures. A wood cabinet with glass windows. A distressed mantel with green tones. Exposed pink brick. White walls. Blue drapes. And a big brown leather sofa, accompanied by gray swivel chairs.

DAVE: *That sounds like the design of a crazy person.*

It does sound like a lot. But if you see the space, you'll note that it feels grounded. And it has a lot to do with the room's big pocket doors, which I painted black. White would be bland, and any other color would be one too many, but black is a solid, classic backdrop—like an accent wall—that matches and ties together everything.

MAKE GOALS INSTEAD OF RESOLUTIONS

There's something about the word "resolution" that doesn't click with me. Just the fact that it has the word "solution" in it implies that there's a problem, and problems make me grumpy. I much prefer the word "goal," which is short, sweet, and totally focused on the future. I used to feel like I was behind the eight ball every New Year's Eve when people would ask about my New Year's resolutions, and I never had one. So one year I decided I was going to get in on the resolution action, boldly announcing to anyone who would listen that I was going to get in the best shape of my life and run my first marathon.

DAVE: *At least you came up with something original. Most people just vow to get in the best shape of their lives and run their first marathon.*

KORTNEY: *I know. I was a walking cliché.*

DAVE: *Actually, you were a running cliché. Strutting into the fancy jogging store, zeroing in like a little blonde laser on the two most expensive pairs of running shoes in the whole store, and buying five matching jogging suits to go with them.*

KORTNEY: *Okay. They weren't jogging "suits."*

DAVE: *What do you call it when your pants, shirt, and jacket all match?*

KORTNEY: *Fine. They were jogging suits.*

I didn't log a single mile in those jogging suits, much less run a marathon. And every time I looked at my shiny expensive shoes, I felt a twinge of guilt.

DAVE: *Just a twinge? Those were $150 shoes.*

KORTNEY: *Maybe more of a mild cramp. But still not enough pain to get me to run.*

The resolution was too big. And my desire to achieve it was too small. And the thing with resolutions is that once you "fail," it's over. *Oh well, so much for that. Pass the Cheetos.*

Just because the calendar has you turning over a new leaf doesn't mean your brain will get the memo. So now I take a different approach.

Every December 31, I sit and reflect on the past year and then write a summary that I can look back on. I revisit the pictures I posted on social media and recall experiences and moments I might otherwise have forgotten. I think about my accomplishments, my disappointments, and what I really (really) want to achieve in the coming year. And I write down some realistic, attainable goals to guide me.

There's something to be said for the reset button a new calendar year provides; and who doesn't love a clean slate? But I prefer to go gently into the new year, with a solid sense of direction rather than a rigid to-do list. I'll set the intention to take more walks, for example. Rather than committing to walk four miles a day, six days a week. Last year, my goals were to eat less dairy and learn to cook more vegan dishes, see more concerts, and spend more time one-on-one with friends. And even though I didn't nail every last one, I fared better than I would have had I not set the goals in the first place. I also ended up running my first 5K. And while it wasn't a marathon, I felt like I'd finally earned those running shoes.

The idea is to set yourself up for progress—not perfection.

TILE IT, DON'T DEFILE IT

It's almost inappropriate how much I love tile. It's versatile, relatively inexpensive, the options are endless, and it can take a kitchen or bathroom from meh to uh-may-zing in no time flat.

Dos and Don'ts of Tile Design

DO take the kitchen backsplash all the way to the ceiling. Not only will it look gorgeous, but it will be infinitely easier to clean after the inevitable annual spaghetti sauce explosion. I'd rather you select a less expensive but still timeless subway tile and take it all the way up the wall than choose a super fancy tile style only to have it fizzle out halfway to the ceiling.

DON'T ever, ever, *ever* end the kitchen backsplash tile before it touches the bottom of the cabinets. Ever. When you leave a space there, angels cry. And nothing stains grout like angel tears, so *don't do it.*

DO consider using larger tiles for high-traffic areas like mudrooms and kitchens. While tile is easy to clean, the porous surface between tiles, otherwise known as grout, is not. Larger tiles means fewer grout lines, and fewer grout lines means less to clean. One exception to this rule

is shower floors. Because the shower pan isn't completely flat, a large-scale tile is more likely to crack or break. Instead, choose a tidy mosaic tile for these uneven floors.

DON'T use white grout on any surface that will be walked on. I don't care what the sealer says on the back of the bottle; it will not save white grout from getting dingy. With kids and pets, your white grout will be gray within a matter of hours, if not minutes.

DO consider the way tile feels. Especially when it comes to floors. You wouldn't buy a carpet without feeling it first, and tile is no different. Your feet are going to touch it several times a day, so don't let the feeling come as a surprise. Smoother tiles work well on bathroom floors, whereas I prefer a rock bottom floor on wet surfaces like the shower. Tile that varies in depth on the wall may give the room added texture, but will it annoy you every time you touch it? I can't answer that for you. Feel it for yourself!

And last but not least, leave the tile for last. Very rarely do I make my tile selections until the cabinets, paint, and lighting are done. That's not because tile is less important to the room,

but because I know how many options there are and I want to get the color and style just right. If I don't like the color of the cabinets, I can paint them. Same with the walls. But once the grout dries, tile is a time-intensive mistake to fix. Before I commit, I always hold up a sheet of tiles next to the cabinets, instead of a single square, so I can really get a feel for it. I'll take a look at it in different lighting and at different times of day to be 100 percent certain the color is speaking to me.

DAVE: *What if you're using tiles in multiple colors and they're all trying to speak to you at once?*

KORTNEY: *I listen with my eyes. And if my eyes are overwhelmed, I dial back the color—or the number of colors—until they work in harmony.*

Because tile is labor intensive, I tend to favor monochromatic or neutral palettes over multi-colored mosaics. Mosaics are cool, but they're also limiting. So I limit them to small accent areas, like an old fireplace, a tabletop, or a small bar backsplash. When it comes to walls and floors, where I'm covering a large area with tile, I prefer to satisfy my color craving with the surrounding decor, which can be easily updated, and allow the tile to serve as an anchor or backdrop.

RELISH THE BLUES

When it comes to exterior house paint, the blues bring me nothing but joy. Blue paired with a bright white trim is always a win.

Navy and dark hues will read as neutrals from the street, while lighter, brighter variations say "all eyes on me."

TELL THE FUTURE YOU'RE NOT INTERESTED IN A RELATIONSHIP RIGHT NOW

I'm a girl who likes to take charge. It's not enough for me just to know what's coming next—I want to *decide* what's coming next, and probably tell it what to do after that. So when life takes my steering wheel away against my will, it can feel like I'm spinning out of control. If you've ever driven a car on black ice, you know the feeling. And while every fiber of your being wants to *resist* the spin, you actually have to turn into it, in order to correct your course. You also have to take your foot off the accelerator and pump the brakes. Gently.

Take the early days of motherhood, for example. Granted, there are plenty of new moms who float around on a cloud of maternal bliss until their kid turns 18, and if you're one of them, good on you. But for some of us, the first few weeks of motherhood can be a bit of a roller coaster. Around the two-week mark of being home with your first child, it may occur to you that you've made a terrible, irreversible error of judgment. This feeling is perfectly normal. You are sleep-deprived. Your hormones are *hormoning*. And to top it all off, this shriveled, needy human has zero regard for your personal space. It's just cry, cry, cry, and take, take, take.

This is when you *must* take your foot off the accelerator. Surrender to the moment right in front of you, and tell the future you're just not interested in a relationship with it right now. Don't even give it a second thought until the fog has lifted.

I have used this technique to get through some very difficult times, and while it's not always easy to do, it's the greatest gift you can give yourself.

BUY THE BEST TABLE YOU CAN AFFORD

When Dave and I bought our first house together, one of our first big purchases was our dining room table. To get a feel for what we might want, we stopped to browse at a trendy furniture store that was way out of our league. Of course, we found the perfect solid wood farm table that was also way out of our league. Or it would have been out of our league had it not been for the store's display of candles, which had left permanent wax rings on the table's surface, rendering it "defective merchandise."

DAVE: *Candles make everything better.*

KORTNEY: *Right?*

One man's defective merchandise is another man's surprisingly affordable dream table. Wax rings, schmax rings—we just covered those puppies up with more candles and called it a win.

Little did we know just how big a win that one investment would be. This table has moved with us twice now, and it still works for us, despite the evolving style of our homes. Why? Because it's a beautifully made, super solid piece of furniture, with great lines. And because it's made of solid pine, we can sand it down and change it up whenever it's time for a change. For the cost of supplies—about $60—and a few hours of work, we get a brand-new table.

DAVE: *Sixty dollars may cover the supplies, but let's not forget you also like to change up the dishes every time you change the color of the table.*

KORTNEY: *True, but you and the kids have a tendency to break, chip, and lose our dishware, so it's usually time to restock anyway. Three times in 14 years is a good deal for you, Wilson.*

How to Refinish, Refresh, Rejoice! (Buy New Dishes!)

1. Use an electric sander with 80-grit sandpaper to sand your tabletop. The goal is to expose the wood and get a nice even surface. Hand-sanding not only takes too long for my liking, but it's very difficult to get the surface as smooth as I want it. Because our table is pine, which is a fairly soft wood, it takes about an hour to remove the top finish. Oak and other hardwoods will take a little longer.

2. Lightly sand the entire table surface with 120-grit sandpaper. Then do the same with 220-grit sandpaper. The higher the grit, the less it penetrates the wood and the more finely it smooths the surface, preparing it to take the stain.

3. Apply stain using a paintbrush, a rag, or both. I usually do both, brushing the stain on in the direction of the wood grain, then massaging it in gently with a rag. The thicker the coat, the darker the color, and while some experts will recommend wiping off any excess stain, you don't have to.

4. Once the stain is dry, lightly sand the stained surface by hand with 220-grit sandpaper. As wood absorbs stain, the fibers expand, making the surface uneven. Hand-sanding restores that even finish. I will typically apply two coats and hand-sand between each one.

5. Once the stain is completely dry (this can take anywhere from two to 24 hours, depending on the stain and the knots in the wood, which can take longer to absorb stain), apply your top coat. Polyurethane or polyacrylic finishes work great. A light sand between coats, again by hand with 220-grit paper, will ensure a smoother end result. It will also remove those tiny air bubbles and imperfections before you apply the next coat. I recommend two to three coats of the clear finish.

6. Pro tip: The finish you choose can affect the resulting color. Ask your local paint store if you can see a sample of the stain and finish on similar wood before you commit to staining your entire table. I overlooked this step the last time I refinished our table, and the polyurethane brought out the yellow in the pine a bit too much for my taste.

7. Allow the table to dry for 24 hours before using it, then enjoy until you get bored. Or until your husband and kids break enough dishes to justify a change in decor.

FACING PAGE: If you have kids, there's a fair chance they will carve something into the table, be it their names or initials, or just a homework assignment where they pressed too hard without putting anything under their paper to protect the table. It used to drive me nuts, but then the last time we went to sand down the table, I saw the words "Jett was here" carved in his five-year-old hand, and I could barely stand to sand them away. Memories are everywhere. Here's Lennox staking her claim on the old table before the recent restoration (*top left*).

TREAT THE CLOSET LIKE THE ROOM IT IS

I do my best not to overthink *anything*. But there is such a thing as underthinking, and I see it all the time when it comes to walk-in closets. If you're lucky enough to have one of these precious rooms, treat it like one. Every time I see a closet groaning under the weight of a thousand hanging garments, I want to call CPS (closet protective services). If only there were such a thing.

DAVE: *There is. Her name is Kortney Wilson.*

If your closet has nothing going for it but hangers, it's time to stage an intervention. Choose a focal point (a charming chandelier, perhaps—or a piece of art or a lovely jewelry cabinet on one wall) and thoughtfully make space for things that don't hang. That means adding shelves. A closet *has* to have shelves. If you hang a clothing rod on every wall (something I see all the time), you are doing yourself—and your wardrobe—a great disservice. You're also inviting the clothes-hanger-challenged members of your family to pile their clothes on the nearest chair and bypass the closet altogether.

DAVE: *Who does that?*

KORTNEY: *Not you, thanks to the abundance of shelves in your closet.*

Dave can't operate a clothes hanger to save his life, but he can triple fold a pair of jeans and place them on top of the other jeans on a shelf.

Personally, I prefer to fold the majority of my clothes and store them on open shelving. Not only is it more visually interesting, it also allows me to take inventory of what I have at a glance. If your wardrobe is fairly sparse, more power to you, but don't forgo the shelves. A piece of art, a stylish hat on a stand, a faux plant (totally acceptable for closets, where you're not trying to fool anyone but yourself), or a handbag, displayed among the clothes, will break up the space and make the closet feel complete.

DAVE WILSON MASTER CLASS
THE ART OF THE APOLOGY

———

The Apology Cake
Delicious and functional. Please note that if the one you've wronged is counting calories, the Apology Fruit Cup is not an acceptable substitute.

Champagne and strawberries
A glass of bubbly and a plate of strawberries delivered on a tray by an adorable child is always a winner. Bonus points if you put the kid in a bow tie. Negative bonus points if your wife just told you that she's given up alcohol for the month of January.

Lipstick on the mirror
This maneuver has a romantic element of surprise, which I love. However, it can only be performed with cheap drugstore lipstick. Using her favorite $40 designer lipstick is a rookie mistake that will require yet another apology.

The serenade
It is almost impossible for Kortney to resist an apology set to music. Especially one that rhymes. "I'm such a louse; I'm in the doghouse. You're so pretty; what I did was . . ." You get the idea.

LANDSCAPE FOR YOUR LIFESTYLE

——

When it comes to real estate, landscaping shapes the first impression, and it can make or break a listing. Framing the house and offering up some outdoor "decor" in the form of greenery, stones, and other hardscape can be the deciding factor of whether a buyer walks into the house at all. As a Realtor, I've seen it time and again. I've been with a family all day, looking at houses, and by the end of the afternoon, they're tired and cranky and I want to show them *just one more*. If we pull up to a house where the landscaping is lame, the potential buyer will assume the inside of the house probably is too, and they pass on what could be the perfect fit. I'm not saying the landscaping has to be fancy or high maintenance—but it should be neat and well kept. Even if your house is not on the market, a tidy exterior is infinitely more pleasant to come home to.

I happen to like landscaping, though no one has ever accused me of having a green thumb. If anything, I'd give myself more of a yellow thumb.

DAVE: *Yellow, like a warning light. Proceed with caution.*

KORTNEY: *Exactly.*

Landscaping is expensive. With a coat of paint, you can make a mistake and it's not the end of the world. With landscaping, you make a mistake, and—

DAVE: *Everything dies.*

Dave and I learned this the hard way. We thought we were saving money by *not* hiring a landscaper and by just following our instincts.

DAVE: *Turns out, our instincts don't know jack about sunlight and soil quality.*

In the long run, not paying for at least a consult probably cost us thousands of dollars.

DAVE: *Not to mention the thousands of flower lives that were lost to our carelessness.*

We've since learned our lesson.

DAVE: *And his name is Jeff.*

KORTNEY: *Aka the Garden Whisperer.*

A good landscaper is a lot like a good therapist. Sure, they know the science of plants and sunlight and soil quality, but they also have to be great listeners. They take time to understand your lifestyle, your strengths and weaknesses, and your skill level, so they can figure out what you're capable of. That way you wind up with a lawn you not only love to look at, but can keep alive.

When our kids were little, they loved to toddle around in the yard for hours while Dave and I dug in the dirt and did our planting. Saturdays were dedicated to yard work, and the kids just thought we were having fun. Now that they've wised up to the "work" aspect of yard work, they want no part of it. They'd rather spend the weekend playing with friends—and frankly, so would Dave and I, if at all possible. So we've shifted our landscaping accordingly.

Landscaper Jeff knows I love to plant a garden every year—all by myself. And he knows I like to see flowers in bloom for as long as possible. He also knows I have a weakness for pink petunias cascading over fences, so he helps me select things that will make me happy without being too high maintenance. And as the warm weather settles in, it's nice to know I don't have to spend weeks getting ready to enjoy it.

If gardening and lawn maintenance aren't your thing, consider leaning more heavily on hardscapes: stones and pavers and walls and other non-botanical features. As much as I love greenery, the soft green grass from my Northern youth is not the same down South. Here the grass is coarse and prone to yellowing in the 100-degree heat. It can survive long summer droughts and armies of annoying insects. I, on the other hand, can't survive armies of annoying insects. Which is why we did away with much of our back lawn a few years ago and replaced it with pavers and a firepit. Now we can play basketball and barbecue and roast marshmallows without getting eaten alive, and we love our backyard again. If the kids want to play soccer or have a picnic in the grass, they do it in the front yard.

Long story short: You have to do what works for you. Landscape around your lifestyle; don't change your lifestyle to match your landscaping. And for goodness' sake, do yourself a favor and hire a Jeff.

HIDE THE TAPE

I like to believe that in heaven, there is a tape dispenser in every room, fully loaded and ready for adhesive action.

DAVE: *You might say it's your death wish.*

KORTNEY: *It definitely gives me something to look forward to.*

In our house, however, a fresh roll of tape disappears faster than a plate of peanut butter cookies. It's like the tape speaks in a high-pitched voice that only children can hear: *Come to me, small people . . . together we can stick this thing to this other thing and make them one.* I never see the fruits of their sticky labor either. I don't know where the tape goes or what they're using it for. I just know that every time I go to wrap a gift, it's gone.

For a while, I took to hiding rolls of tape in drawers around the house where the kids wouldn't think to look. But the tape called to them: *I'm in your mother's makeup drawer and I'm lonely and no one understands me but youuuuu.* The kids, hearing this, no doubt stopped whatever they were doing and started taping each other's eyelids shut.

So, I had to up my game.

This tactic works especially well if you have young boys who want nothing to do with your mystifying stash of lady supplies. And to be extra safe, the tampons help muffle the tape's siren song so the kids can barely hear it.

Happy gift wrapping!

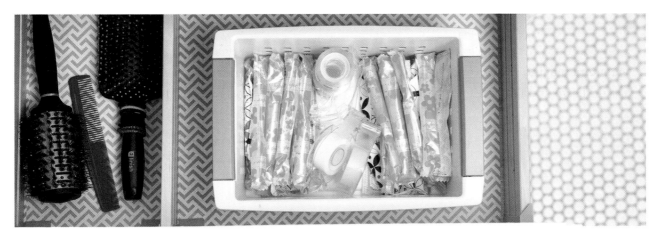

BE A "SOME" BODY

When I was young and had nothing but my own dreams to attend to, fitness was one of my top priorities. I did yoga, lifted weights, and got my daily dose of cardio. I was defined—literally and figuratively—by the shape my body was in. My happiness and my appearance went hand in hand, like sorority sisters during pledge week. *Squeee! You're so pretty! No, you're so pretty! I'm so happy we're both so pretty!* You could toss a Canadian quarter at my abs, and the higher it bounced, the greater was my self-worth. This is not an earth-shattering revelation, I know. It's pretty much the female experience in a nutshell. But the way I approach fitness has changed quite a bit since my younger years, and while my abs are no longer rock solid, my confidence is on far less shaky ground. You're going to hate me for it, but the secret really is *moderation*.

I know. Moderation is the worst! I want to punch the idea of it in the face. But when your life expands to include a partner and children and a career, your definition of exercise may need to expand also. I've found that in order to keep fitness in my routine, I've had to abandon the "all or nothing" approach and embrace the concept of "some." (Side note: this also works with jelly beans, which is annoying but true.)

If you will give yourself permission to be a "some" body instead of an "all or nothing" body, you can enjoy better health and greater sanity—in less than 15 minutes a day. Now, please understand: I'm not telling you to abandon a more rigorous fitness routine if that's what works for you. I'm really talking to the people who think, *Some day I'll have time to* really *get in shape, but until then, pass me the remote.* Some is better than none.

BRUSH AND SQUAT

Every morning while I brush my teeth, I do squats. I use an electric toothbrush and let it go to town on my smile for two minutes while I bob up and down like a lunatic. (You might want to close the bathroom door for this. Or you might enjoy scaring the kids, like I do.)

PEPPER IN SOME PUSHUPS

You don't have to do them all at once to reap the rewards. Personally, I like to do three sets of 20 and spread them out over the day. Waiting for a conference call to start? Imagine a tiny drill sergeant standing on your shoulder (mine wears tight shorts and a whistle), and drop and give him 20. Or 10. Or five if that's all you have time for. It's really about training

your brain to admit that *some* exercise feels better than *no exercise*. (And once your brain gets the memo, you'll likely find yourself craving a few extra reps.)

TEACH AB-RITHMETIC

I keep a big blue exercise ball in the kids' playroom, which doubles as our homeschool classroom. Maybe it's some holdover from my childhood, but it's so shiny and bouncy, I literally can't resist sitting on it. So I sit on it while I'm working with Sully or Lennox as they do math. And since I'm already sitting there, I'll do a set of 10 crunches while they work out a problem. And then I'll do another set. And another. Because it's math time and I know that these little sets *add up*.

WALK AND TALK

There's been so much written recently about how bad sitting is for your body. I'm grateful that my work doesn't require long hours behind a desk, but I'm not exactly an aerobics instructor either. Between my real estate business and filming the show, I'm on my feet more than most—and I try to keep that up even when I'm not shooting or showing houses. For example, I rarely just talk on the phone, I *walk* on the phone. Even if it means pacing back and forth in the kitchen, walking and talking keeps me focused on the conversation and keeps the blood flowing. If Donnie is sitting by the front door clearly jonesing for some quality time, I'll grab the leash and take my phone on the road. The fresh air is medicine for my soul, and the extra movement does wonders for my mood.

WATCH AND WEIGHT LIFT

I'm a sucker for hand weights in candy colors. It's like my brain thinks I'm going to get to eat them when the workout is over. Whatever works, right? That's why I keep a set of these cute little weights near the television, so when I do have an opportunity to catch up on my favorite shows, they call to me: *Just a couple of reps, Kortney . . . be a "some" body, Kortney.* Sometimes I scream "wrong number!" and hide under a blanket. But more often than not, I answer the call, do 10 reps, and my arms are better for it.

While none of these micro workouts alone would qualify to most as "exercise," at this point in my life, it all adds up—without me having to add exercise to my calendar.

EAT THE PANTRY

I hate to waste food. So once every couple of months, I announce it's time to eat the pantry and I refuse to buy any nonessential groceries until everything is gone. Canned goods, snack crackers, frozen meals, fruits and vegetables that are going untouched—even if it's not *technically* in the pantry, if it's edible, it's got to be eaten.

DAVE: *The kids hate eating the pantry.*

KORTNEY: *I'm aware.*

DAVE: *You make them eat old apples.*

KORTNEY: *They don't have to eat them. They can juice them or throw them in a Crock-Pot and make applesauce, or they could bake them in a pie.*

DAVE: *Um, have you met our kids?*

KORTNEY: *Yeah. They're the ones in the pantry, eating soon-to-be-rotten apples, right?*

DAVE: *That's them!*

No one loves eat-the-pantry time, but it forces me to get creative with meal planning, and I kind of like the challenge.

DAVE: *Sully refers to those meals as "Everything but the Kitchen Sink Meals."*

KORTNEY: *Well, when Sully has to spend his own money on food, maybe he'll appreciate the days when he had "everything but the kitchen sink" to eat. For free.*

DAVE: *Doubtful. But it's a cute thought.*

I understand that there will always be *some* waste, but this process is one teeny-tiny way we can reduce our carbon footprint—and appreciate the food we've bought with our hard-earned money. Even if we have to put up with a few bad apples.

DAVE: *Are you talking about the kids or the actual apples?*

KORTNEY: *I guess you'll never know.*

CLEAN BEFORE SLEEP

———

They say the secret to a happy marriage is "never go to bed angry." I say the secret to a happy marriage is "never go to bed angry that you didn't clean up first." It has a nice ring to it, no?

DAVE: *No.*

Nevertheless. Nothing stifles my will to live like waking up to post-party mayhem. It's a new day, and I want it to look like one. That's why after the last guest departs, no matter what the hour, you'll find me scurrying around, picking up trash, vacuuming floors, spraying down surfaces, and waving off those pesky divorce papers that Dave keeps thrusting into my determined face.

DAVE: *Those weren't divorce papers. They were mental health pamphlets. Because I care.*

KORTNEY: *Well, I recycled them, along with the beer cans and paper plates.*

As much as I'd like to be the laid-back, "it'll all get done in good time" type, I'm just not wired that way.

DAVE: *You're wired more like an electric fence. "DON'T TOUCH ME UNTIL WE'RE DONE CLEANING."*

KORTNEY: *Let me ask you this, Dave. Have you ever woken up after a party and regretted my need to clean the night before?*

DAVE: *Never.*

KORTNEY: *Then I rest my case.*

While the rest of you married couples can stay up and fight, I'd rather Dave go to bed angry that I made him clean, so we can both wake up happy in the morning.

LETTING GO IS NOT THE SAME AS QUITTING

One of the hardest decisions I ever had to make was the decision to stop pursuing a career in music. Quitting has never been part of my vocabulary, and music was my first love. It was the reason I moved to Nashville at 18, knowing no one, with less than $200 to my name. There was no doubt in my mind back then that I would "make it" in the music business. Within a week of moving to Nashville, I was offered a publishing deal and a production deal with Starstruck Entertainment. Reba McEntire—one of my heroes—and her then husband, Narvel Blackstock, owned Starstruck, and Reba thought I showed promise and gave me backing through Starstruck to record. When I was signed to Lyric Street Records eight weeks later, I felt like it was meant to be.

For three years, the stars were aligned. I was in what we affectionately refer to in Nashville as the "Artist Protection Program." I received an advance on future sales, rushed into the studio to make a record, and then . . . waited for two years until it was "my turn" to come out. The publishing deal meant I got paid to write songs, though I had never written before. The hope

was that I'd cowrite something and eventually record it. It was like we were filling the well for the future. I'd meet different cowriters (some of them the most successful in Nashville) in the mornings and then again in the afternoons for writing sessions. It was exciting but also confusing. I'd come to Nashville to sing. But now that I had a record deal, I was just writing and waiting. In fact, I wasn't even allowed to perform in bars, which I had come to town completely prepared to do. I just had to sit tight.

Two years went by and then I got the call from the label that it was time to go on a radio tour to promote my record. Four days later I was flying across the country, visiting up to three cities a day, and meeting with radio stations, essentially begging them to play my records. I'd have breakfast in Philly, lunch in New York City, and dinner in Connecticut. I was burning out fast, but I knew this was the name of the game, and there was no way I was going to show the toll it was taking on me. Amid all this was the Country Radio Seminar (otherwise known as CRS), which is when all of the radio stations descend on Nashville and set up camp in different hotel rooms and studios to meet with artists—both new ones like myself and very accomplished ones. I met with the stations from sunup to sundown, doing interviews, promoting the record, and recording "record liners" for future use: "This is Kortney Wilson and you're listening to WXYZ Radio."

The day after my first CRS, I could barely keep my eyes open, but I was scheduled to fly to Cincinnati to promote my record. The label called a last-minute meeting in the early morning, just hours before my scheduled departure. It seemed odd, but honestly, I was so exhausted, it barely registered. Then they said they were pulling my single from radio the next day. Instead, they wanted to push a single from a new band they'd just signed called Rascal Flatts. I was devastated. Not only that, but I still had to fly to Cincinnati and fulfill my obligation to the radio station, which meant pumping gas on air, broadcasting remotely from a local gas station. This is what new artists do on radio to show appreciation to the station for playing their songs. I smiled through it, but inside, I was wrecked.

When I got back, I asked to be released from my record deal. I was coming up on three and a half years and didn't want to release music that old, *if* my number ever came up. I wanted to pursue opportunities with other labels. It was a bold move, but it felt right—and I was in talks to sign with a new label before I even played my last show for Lyric Street Records. That show was part of a summer concert series in New York City, and I opened for none other than Rascal Flatts. It was early September 2001, and we performed on a stage set between the Twin Towers.

One week later, the Twin Towers fell. And on the morning of September 11, as I sat watching the devastation on television, the president of the new label called to tell me they would not be able to sign me after all. I was numb to that news, overcome with emotion over the much larger story developing before my eyes.

I was never again signed as a solo artist. But at the time, I was too overwhelmed to see it as the ending it was. I saw it as a setback that Dave and I would overcome together. He lost his record deal shortly after that—and because I've always been driven by a strong sense of destiny, I guess I saw it as a sign that we weren't meant to have solo careers. Maybe we were meant to be a duo.

Opportunity came knocking for us again, this time as The Wilsons, when we were signed to Sony Music Canada. Once you've had a taste of success, it's that much harder to let the dream go. Especially in the music business, where your luck—for better or for worse—can turn on a dime. Dave and I were writing and recording and performing at festivals here and there, and we knew that one song could launch us. But we had three kids at this point, and while I didn't want to give up on my dreams, I had dreams for my family as well, and the uncertainty of a career in music made me uncomfortable. Also, I was tired. Dave and I weren't enjoying the process the way we once had. It felt like we were putting everything into it and getting nothing out. I had been pursuing music since I was

11 years old, and here I was, at age 30, having visions of myself at 40, singing demos and jingles to pay the bills. I didn't want to disappoint all the people who had believed in me, but my gut instinct said it was time to let it go. And Dave felt the same way. The only question left was, *What in the hell would we do next?*

DAVE: *Gut instincts give terribly non-specific career advice. They're all "You guys should totally get out of the music business and just, like . . . you know."*

I had no idea what I should—or even *could*—do next. I considered everything from marketing to medicine, narrowing my focus to careers that wouldn't require another four to eight years of school. We were flipping one house a year at this point, to supplement our income. I liked houses. I loved design. And I knew, having been in the entertainment industry, I was perfectly capable of marketing myself. So I made the most practical decision of my life so far and pursued my real estate license.

It seemed like a logical next step that would afford me a flexible schedule and eventually the kind of lifestyle I wanted for our family. I surrendered to this new way of life—and realized pretty quickly how liberating it was to have a career selling something other than myself.

And then, in little ways, music and performing started making their way back to me. I took on the talent show at the kids' elementary school and got to watch and cheer as young performers took the stage for the very first time. I joined the board of a children's theater company, which is where it all began for me, playing Annie in a local production in my early teens. A friend from my early days in Nashville still calls from time to time and asks, albeit bashfully, for me to record jingles for him. I love it! I don't need the money, and my ego's not wrapped up in it. It's just 100 percent pure fun. And occasionally, when Dave and I are doing a speaking engagement, someone in the audience will ask me to sing. I'll do a verse and a chorus, and I love watching the surprised looks from fans who didn't know music was a part of my story.

On the one hand, it makes me miss my music days. On the other, it's so liberating to sing purely for the joy of it and not because I need the crowd's approval. These days I know they've come to see me for a completely different reason, and the singing is just a fun surprise—something extra I can give people without needing anything in return.

It took some living to realize that I never really gave up on music; I just stopped pursuing it as a career, which gave me the freedom and space to fall in love with it again in new and surprising ways.

Every time music pokes its head into my life and whispers in my ear, I wonder what will become of the two of us. And wondering is just enough to keep the love alive.

YOU CAN'T HAVE IT ALL . . .

I've got to give props to Oprah, who in an interview once said, "You can have it all, but not all at once." My inner protest marcher *hated* this advice. She immediately started picketing the television:

—*WHAT DO WE WANT?*
—*IT ALL!*
—*WHEN DO WE WANT IT?*
—*NOW!*

But my older, wiser inner self knew that there was wisdom in this advice. And also? *Permission.* "You can have it all, but not all at once" was the permission I needed to live more than one life in my lifetime. To choose being a stay-at-home mom today and know that it wouldn't keep me from pursuing a career tomorrow.

Dave and I have reinvented ourselves countless times—trading in one way of life for another. It gives me so much comfort to be able to model this for my kids. "You *can* have it all. You just can't have it all at once."

LOVE YOUR LIGHTING

———

Think of light fixtures as the jewelry of your home. While it might be the last thing you put on, don't treat it like an afterthought. There was a time when Dave and I overlooked the aesthetic importance of lighting, treating it as a mere technicality. We'd hit the clearance section and take what we could get—even if a fixture was a little too small (or a little too ugly), we figured it was the last thing people noticed. And we were wrong.

While they don't have to be a room's focal point, gorgeous fixtures certainly can be. When deciding how large a fixture to buy, the rule of thumb is to add the length and width of your room and convert to inches. So if the room is 12 by 12 feet, the fixture should be 24 inches (60 centimeters) in diameter. Personally, I like to add a couple of inches for good measure.

DAVE: *If I were less of a gentleman, I could make a joke there.*

KORTNEY: *Way to restrain yourself.*

Better to err on the side of "go big or go home" than on "fixture, what fixture?" Especially in smaller rooms. Contrary to conventional wisdom, smaller rooms are great candidates for larger-scale fixtures, which will bring focus and double as a work of art (for significantly less cost—and wall space—than an original painting).

Ambient, Accent, and Task Lighting

If light fixtures are the jewelry of the home, *light* is like makeup, bringing warmth and dimension to a space, highlighting certain areas and downplaying others. One kind of light can't do this work alone. Every room needs a blend of ambient, accent, and task lighting to feel complete.

Ambient lights are your overheads (chandeliers or recessed lights, typically the room's main light sources), which I like to have on a dimmer switch. Accent lights are typically side lamps set on nightstands or console tables. And task lighting is just what it sounds like: a more focused light intended—and directed—for a certain task (often reading).

Funny story. When I visited my sister last year and decided to do a 24-hour makeover of her master bedroom, lighting played a big part in the transformation. I had painted the space and piled on new pillows and linens, but what really made my sister's eyes pop was the lighting. The room looked bigger, and brighter, but also—according to my sister and brother-in-law—more romantic. *That* is the magic of ambient, accent, and task lighting. Previously their room had had one overhead light. I added two side lamps on either side of the bed, and one on the console table (accent). I placed one curved lamp over the love seat to create a reading area (task), and then I put the overhead light on a dimmer switch, for mood lighting (ambient).

When we revealed the room to my sister and her four little boys, the kids jumped all over the room saying how much they loved it. Then my four-year-old nephew pointed to the corner of the room and said, "Mommy, what's that?" She kept asking what he was pointing to, and then he described "where the light is coming from."

When we realized he was talking about the lamp, we started laughing. There was light in every room of their house, but not a single lamp.

My sister is not someone who believes in excess, and because there was plenty of light in her house, it never occurred to her to go out and buy a bunch of lamps. But once she saw how blended lighting transformed the mood and feel of the room, and gave her the flexibility to dial it up and dial it down depending on the time of day—well, I guess you could say she saw the light.

Start by focusing on ambience. You can accomplish it easily by putting your primary fixture on a dimmer switch. You don't even have to change out the fixture you have now (unless it's ugly—in which case, take this opportunity to upgrade).

Next you want to light up those dark corners. If you're in renovation mode, consider adding recessed lighting closer to the edges and corners of the room, or even under built-in shelves (the ones that go floor to ceiling, of course). You can also use recessed lighting to highlight a fireplace or a piece of art, and this will check the "accent lighting" box in much the same way a lamp would.

Finally, address your task lighting. I often use free-standing or table lamps for this purpose if it's in a living room, and built-in task lighting in the kitchen. Task lighting is also essential in the bathroom, particularly for makeup application, in which case I'll use pendant lights or sconces. If you've ever tried to put makeup on in a hotel bathroom with low overhead light and no windows, you've probably emerged looking like a child of the '80s. Forgo the trowel, please, and trust me when I say, *Invest in task lighting in your own bathroom.* It will save you a fortune on powder and foundation.

TAKE THE FRIENDSHIP TEST

A sense of humor is one of the qualities I value most in a friend, for sure. The ability to curse like a truck driver and speak the unvarnished truth doesn't hurt either. But there's one thing that sets my core group of friends apart from all the rest: they are happiest when I'm happy. I have always said that the true test of friendship happens not when you're down in the dumps but when you're up in the clouds. When life is going really well, are your friends there to support you? It's human nature to step in when things are bad, but when all is well, and I'm happy and settled, my real friends are the ones who settle in and are happy for me.

LOSE THE BATTLE
TO WIN THE WAR

———

If I were advising Dave on this subject, especially when it comes to design, I'd say that now is *always* the right time to compromise. But sometimes even I need to lose a fight in order to win overall. Car shopping is one of those times. There are few shopping experiences less pleasant than shopping for a car. The schmoozing, the haggling, the fact that the purchase process takes an entire day regardless of how quickly you come to a decision. Just take my money and give me the keys! It doesn't have to be this difficult.

Dave, on the other hand, loves to wheel and deal—and he's good at it.

DAVE: *I definitely don't love it. But I am good at it.*

KORTNEY: *I think you secretly love it.*

DAVE: *I think you need to believe I secretly love it in order to minimize your guilt about making me go car shopping alone.*

KORTNEY: *I don't feel guilty about making you go car shopping alone.*

DAVE: *Why not?*

KORTNEY: *Because I know how much you love it.*

DAVE: *Oh.*

KORTNEY: *See?*

DAVE: *Wait. What just happened?*

So here's where the compromise comes in. Because I would rather eat my own eyeballs with a spork than spend another day of my life at a car dealership, I am willing to compromise on things like make, model, and color. I'll list my preferences, but knowing Dave's the one who has to negotiate, I'm willing to accept that whatever car he comes home with won't check *all* of my boxes.

Actually, not only do I accept it, *I can pretty much count on it.*

DAVE: *You're still bitter about the green Kia.*

KORTNEY: *I just thought when I said "any car but a Kia, any color but green," it might steer you in a different direction.*

DAVE: *But who got an amazing deal on a green Kia?*

KORTNEY: *You did, honey.*

When we went to sell the Kia a few years later, I was adamant that I did not want to replace it with a minivan. Especially a red or burgundy one.

DAVE: *But then who got an amazing deal on a minivan?*

KORTNEY: *A burgundy minivan, no less.*

DAVE: *It was maroon.*

See what I mean? Compromise.

EVERYTHING COMES FULL CIRCLE

Dave and I have done a lot of reality television. I think that's hard for some people to get past when they don't know us very well, because—ironically—nothing sounds more fake and contrived than "reality" TV. They must wonder what kind of people would want to live part of their lives in front of a camera. But people who know us well and have watched our shows (often after getting to know us) will tell you that Kortney and Dave on TV aren't a whole lot different than Kortney and Dave at home on the couch, watching TV. We're comfortable in front of the camera, and we have fun with it. But it's entertainment, not acting—and that's hard to understand if you're not in it.

When we were shooting our first show, *Meet the Wilsons*, it was all about Dave and me raising kids and pursuing a career in country music. And it was so much fun. Sully was two and Jett was four, and we were weeks away from the birth of our adopted daughter. Having been through a failed adoption, this was an especially emotional time for us—and I was adamant that there'd be no filming at the hospital when Lennox was born. At the same time, I welcomed the opportunity to capture her homecoming on camera, because it basically amounted to the best home movie ever, and Lennox will always have it to look back on.

What people saw of us on television was very much the real deal, but it wasn't the whole deal. Behind the scenes, while we were filming the show, another mother's story was also unfolding. Lennox was just eight weeks old when the adoption agency called to tell me about a birth mother I'll call Rose,* who was meeting with two adoptive families near Nashville and needed a place to stay for a week while she decided which family she wanted to adopt her baby. I immediately said yes.

DAVE: *And I immediately said, "You're insane."*

---

*The names in this section have been changed to protect the privacy of these individuals.

KORTNEY: *Everyone did. But I was going with my gut. It felt like the right thing to do. And it was only for a week.*

DAVE: *Sure, it was.*

Rose and her two-year-old son, Jonah, came to stay with us a week later. She was five months pregnant at the time. We didn't have a lot of money, but having just adopted Lennox, I felt a deep connection to this woman who was choosing adoption for her baby and giving this enormous, selfless gift, as Lennox's birth mother had done for me. Dave watched Jonah when Rose went to meet the first family. They lived way out in the country with no cell phone

service, and I could tell it made Rose uncomfortable. The second family she went to meet had six children already, all homeschooled in a very strict speak-only-when-spoken-to environment. She couldn't see *herself* living with these families for two weeks, much less her unborn baby. But those were her only options. Rose came back from that second home visit in tears, and without even saying a word between us, Dave and I looked at each other and knew what we wanted to do. We invited Rose to stay with us for the remainder of her pregnancy so she and the adoption agency might have time to figure things out. She tearfully accepted.

That moment was the beginning of a friendship that continues to this day—and it reminds me to always trust my gut instinct, which was the only thing I had to guide me at that time.

As Rose settled in to our home, she and Jonah became a part of our family. And naturally, she began to spend time with our friends. My best friend at the time, Laura, had, like us, gone through a painful failed adoption. The agency that placed Rose with us knew Laura—but said that Rose was adamant about adopting to a family of color, so Laura and her husband, who were white, were not being considered.

As the weeks went on, though, and Rose spent more time with us and with Laura, she started to have a change of heart.

Twelve weeks later, I had the privilege to be in the delivery room as Rose's labor coach and friend, when she gave birth to the baby boy for whom she chose adoption. On the same day, Laura and her husband became that baby's parents.

Leaving the hospital with Rose—*without her baby*—and returning home to my adopted daughter was one of the most profoundly moving moments of my life. I saw firsthand the strength and selflessness and resilience behind Rose's choice, and the wave of emotion and gratitude nearly knocked me off my feet. Rose was not a mother "giving up" her baby. She was a woman, much stronger than I was, giving another woman the chance to become a mother. She wanted a life for her child that she was unable to give him, and her love was so strong that she could push through her own anguish and depression to give him the life she wanted him to have.

When we got back to our house after leaving the hospital, I had no idea what to say to her. She went to her room and closed the door. About an hour later, I knocked on her door and said, "Wanna go out to eat or shop or have coffee or cry or have a pedicure or do anything you want to do?" "Yes," she said. Over steaming bowls of pasta at the Macaroni Grill, she asked me to make her laugh, and I did.

Rose stayed with us for five more weeks before returning home. She was suffering deeply from postpartum depression, her milk had come in, and her body needed to heal. She and Jonah sat quietly upstairs and out of the way of the chaos as we continued filming *Meet the Wilsons*, now as a family of five, thanks to the quiet strength of another birth mother like Rose.

I am eternally grateful for Rose, and for Lennox's birth mother, and for all the women who have chosen adoption—whether giving the gift or receiving it. This full-circle moment changed the way I look at my life and the people in it. It is a constant reminder to me that we are all connected. And that whatever story you're telling—or seeing—it's never the whole story. Like a circle, it's always to be continued.

ACKNOWLEDGMENTS

———

Writing a book is a team effort—and we had the very best team. We are so grateful to the family and friends who cheered us to the finish line, and who continue to shower us with love and high fives (and the occasional underwater breathing apparatus) when we find ourselves feeling like we're way over our heads.

Karrie Galerno, you are the best role model a girl could ask for. Instead of making me feel crazy for taking on yet another project, you have always made me feel strong and capable. You and Dad built the foundation that has allowed me to take chances, believe in myself, learn from my mistakes, accept my failures, and get back on my feet. I love you.

Kate Cassaday, our editor and voice of reason, your vision, guidance, and good humor were absolutely vital to these two newbie authors—and we can't thank you enough for encouraging us to take on this challenge. You are a gift.

Amanda O'Brien, you are a bright light. Dave and I could not have done this without you—literally. Thank you for being our sounding board and story whisperer, and for helping us find just the right words while staying true to who we are. Your humor and friendship are invaluable.

Linda Edell Howard, you have our backs, our fronts, and all of the angles we haven't thought of yet. You are a goddess of logistics and one hell of an attorney. We are so grateful to have you in our corner.

Jake Eichorn, my right-hand man, it is a joy to work with you every day. Thank you for double-checking the details, doing life with a smile, and always knowing when a brookie from Sweet 16th will save the day. You're one of the good ones.

Mike Rilstone, your eye for photography and your passion for keeping it real were exactly what this project needed. Thank you for always being in the right place, at the right time, with the right attitude, and for capturing us so beautifully in our natural habitat.

Catherine Rector, Marcie Anderson, and Angela Ewing, your amazing work staging houses on seasons one, two, and three of *Masters of Flip* was transformative. Thank you.

And last, but certainly not least, to our fans. Your love and support over the years has meant more to us than you will ever know. The combination of your uplifting posts, your words of encouragement, and your ability to make us feel heard through your likes and comments on social media is the heartbeat of our career. This is for you.